Boston's Haunted History

Exploring the Ghosts and Graves of Beantown

By Christopher Forest

Pictures by Melissa R. Forest

Schiffer Publishing Ltd

4880 Lower Valley Road • Atglen, PA 19310

Published by Schiffer Publishing, Ltd.
4880 Lower Valley Road
Atglen, PA 19310
Phone: (610) 593-1777; Fax: (610) 593-2002
E-mail: Info@schifferbooks.com

For our complete selection of fine books on this and related subjects, please visit our website at
www.schifferbooks.com. You may also write for a free catalog.

This book may be purchased from the publisher. Please try your bookstore first.

We are always looking for people to write books on new and related subjects. If you have an idea for
a book, please contact us at *proposals@schifferbooks.com*

Schiffer Publishing's titles are available at special discounts for bulk purchases for sales promotions
or premiums. Special editions, including personalized covers, corporate imprints, and excerpts can be
created in large quantities for special needs. For more information, contact the publisher.

Other Schiffer Books on Related Subjects
Ghosts of Valley Forge and Phoenixville, 978-0-7643-2633-2, $14.95
Baltimore's Harbor Haunts, 978-0-7643-2304-0, $14.95
Schiffer Publishing has a wide selection of books on the paranormal activity of cities around the region.
Please visit our website to learn more.

Copyright © 2008 by Christopher Forest
Library of Congress Control Number: 2007936949

Designed by Mark David Bowyer
Type set in Bard / NewsGoth BT

ISBN: 978-0-7643-2874-9
Printed in the United States of America

Contents

Dedication

This book is dedicated to my lovely wife, Melissa, whose time, patience, and photographic efforts helped make this book become a reality.

It is also dedicated to my family, particularly my parents, Bob and Sandi; brother, Mark, and sister, Debbie, who helped inspire my curiosity of the unknown at an early age.

Finally, I'd like to dedicate this book to Brighid Forest, a beautiful daughter, who was born while I was writing this book. Happy haunting little one.

Acknowledgments

I t takes a village to make a book. There is no doubt about that. Truly, there are many people who were involved with this book who are owed a great deal of thanks.

First, to Dinah Roseberry, a wonderful editor, who eagerly gave me the opportunity to write this book and was a cheerleader from the very start. Thanks for giving me my chance.

I would also like to thank Jennifer Marie Savage, another wonderful editor, whose keen eye helped make this book materialize.

Also, a debt of gratitude goes to my wife, Melissa Forest, who not only took the photographs for this book, but also followed me on many a chase for stories contained in this volume.

Special thanks also goes to Jim McCabe, a bona-fide ghost expert if there ever was one in Boston. He helped me realize that I was indeed on the right track as I pieced together this book.

And, finally, a special thanks also goes to Valerie Wilcox of the National Park Service who informed me about recent hauntings on the Boston Harbor Islands.

Without all of you, this book never would have been possible.

Introduction

B oston. The name conjures up a variety of images. Puritans flocking to the land for religious freedom—and the persecution of witches, pirates, and others who did not quite fit in with Puritan beliefs. Boston was also a hotbed of activity for the Sons of Liberty, tea-dumpers, and America's fight for freedom—and provided early glimpses of the abolitionism, industrialism, and spiritualism movements that were to follow. And, finally, there are the great sports teams known far and wide for their prowess... or lack thereof.

For more than 350 years, America's beloved Beantown (Boston) has held a special spot in American history. Whether it's being a hub of academia, a home to sports fans, or a "beacon upon a hill" as the old-time Puritans used to say, Boston has made its mark in America's history.

It should, then, be of no surprise that Boston not only has its share of historical firsts and footnotes, but has also been a major center of ghostly activity since the first Europeans stepped foot on the land in the early 1600s. The city neighborhoods, cozy side streets, and an array of islands are a treasure trove of ghost stories. Early shipwrecks, famous battles, and an assortment of unique buildings have captured an essence of the past, giving fodder to these stories.

From ghostly sailors, to heartbroken lovers, to not quite dead famous writers and poets, Boston is home to countless ghosts whose stories have been told for nearly three hundred years. You are encouraged to share in these stories and become a part of them. The pages ahead are dedicated to the ghosts found only in Boston that have been gleaned from an assortment of wonderful books, magazines, newspaper articles, and websites. No stone has been left unturned to find these local legends and urban myths that loom like shadows in Boston.

As you will see, Boston's ghost stories are often linked to unique pieces of American history and are best appreciated in the context of this history. Interspersed with the ghostly tales you will read its history. Hopefully, the background behind these stories will help you gain a true understanding – and enjoyment – of them.

Boston not only has many sites to see, but many unseen sites as well. Ghosts roam throughout numerous sections of the city. Some still remain there to this day while others have moved on to new locations or totally disappeared over the years. But all of them will make you stand up and take notice… and perhaps the next time you're in Boston, you might just encounter one of these legendary figures. Or perhaps you will find a new one of your own.

So buckle your seatbelts, put on your ghost-hunting gear, and get ready to see some of Boston's finest legends.

Happy reading!

Author's Note

The stories contained in this book are a composite of many tales told throughout the years. They attempt to capture a glimpse of Boston's haunted past for nearly three centuries.

Many of the places that are mentioned in this book still exist. Some, however, no longer have the public access that they may have once enjoyed. A variety of spots that were once open to tourists are now businesses or private buildings. Some of the islands that are mentioned no longer allow visitors, and the cemeteries that are listed have strict visiting rules.

Ghost enthusiasts are a fun group. However, we ask that if you decide to learn more about these haunts for yourself, that you respect the privacy of those haunts that have now turned into businesses or personal residences and property, as well respect the rules of the islands and cemeteries that dot the city.

Happy hunting.

Boston Common has been an important landmark since British colonists arrived in Boston. More than a few ghosts are said to inhabit the common.

Part One:

One if by Land

oston's landscape is filled with many historic buildings and landmarks old and new. Some of these buildings have existed in the city for more than three hundred years and have a wild assortment of stories of their own to tell. Others, while surviving only a short time, also have developed some unique stories. If only those walls could talk...

A city that has seen layers of history is bound to attract some unearthly visitors. From the famous Boston Common, to theaters, hotels, and dormitories, Boston has captured the spirits of the past and kept them alive and well.

Nearly every street you wander in Boston has a building with an interesting history to it. Here are just a few.

Two Victorian-era ladies reportedly haunt Boston Common.
They are occasionally seen passing this fountain.

The Boston Athenaeum

The Haunted Library...

The History

One of the most unique buildings in Boston is nestled near the Boston State House. It is an attractive looking building called the Boston Athenaeum. Constructed in the 1840s, the building was the brain child of Edward Clarke Cabot, who designed an institution that he hoped would match the fine art that would be displayed inside. Cabot intended the building to rival the Lyceum and Athenaeum of Liverpool, England that was a popular spot at the time.

The building became the home of a large library that was actually founded much earlier, in 1807. The library was dedicated to maintaining a collection of art and literature for the public, as well as private members, to enjoy. The library enjoyed a nomadic existence for its first forty-three years before settling into a building on Pearl Street. It has moved since and is currently located near Boston Common, a bustling boulevard in the heart of Boston.

Shortly after opening in the mid 1800s, the Athenaeum became a stop for some of the most enlightened thinkers to grace the state of Massachusetts. Poets like Henry Wadsworth Longfellow and Transcendentalists like Henry David Thoreau visited the Athenaeum many a day to read books, share ideas, and socialize.

The building is a remarkable testament to the wit and wisdom of the Bay State as well as the United States. More than 700,000 volumes grace the shelves of the library. Some of the interesting items include an early King James Bible, the paintings of John Singer Sargeant and Gilbert Stuart, sculptures of George Washington and Benjamin Franklin, as well as personal artifacts from George Washington.

The Mystery

The Boston Athenaeum has long been a hub of art, literacy, and knowledge in the city. It has served as a tourist spot for literary and philosophic minds. Yet, it also seems to be the home of a bit more. Many visitors have reported that ghosts may grace the halls of the hallowed building.

For more than a century, the main ghost story of the Athenaeum has permeated the streets of Boston. This story begins with an interesting painting of a once famous reverend named Thadeus M. Harris. A frequent visitor, Harris was said to be devoted to the Athenaeum.

According to some sources, Harris's picture is not the only object to remain in the building. His spirit does as well. First mention of Harris's ghost dates back to the days of novelist Nathaniel Hawthorne (whose own ghost is sometimes claimed to inhabit the famous House of Seven Gables in Salem). Like Harris, Hawthorne was a frequent visitor to the library—and he supposedly witnessed the ghost of Reverend Thadeus Harris navigating the corridors of the staid building in April 1842. According the Hawthorne, the ghost first appeared in the Athenaeum shortly after Harris's death. Hawthorne claimed the ghost visited the Athenaeum for six weeks, and often sat at a table reading a newspaper. He and the ghost spent time together in reverent silence, often noticing each other, but never speaking. Ironically,

Hawthorne realized that the ghost of the deceased reverend never paid attention to anyone else on the floor... and no one seemed to notice the departed reverend, either. Somehow, only Hawthorne had the privilege to see the former clergyman. What Hawthorne saw to this day is unknown, but he was said to be so taken by the episode that he used it as the inspiration for his short story, "The Ghost of Dr. Harris."

Athenaeum goers still report sightings of a ghost waiting for an elevator to take to the third floor. Most people believe this to be the ghost of the reverend that Hawthorne saw many years ago. What makes the current encounters even more unique is that the current Athenaeum is no longer housed in the building that Hawthorne or Harris frequented. The library was moved from that Pearl Street location to its present day location near the Boston Common decades ago. However, it would appear that didn't stop dear Reverend Harris from following the books and moving to the new library. Many people think that Harris still rides an elevator to the third floor, so many years after he last visited the old building.

Boston Common

America's Haunted Common...

The History

In 1628 William Blackstone migrated to America. He left his English life behind and boarded a ship sailing to the colony near Plymouth, Massachusetts. Upon his arrival, hoping to find solitude in the wilderness of the New World, he set off north, toting his own personal belongings and a small library of books.

Blackstone found a perfect spot to live amid a grassy plain in a region local Native Americans called Shawmut. He was accepted by the Native Americans and soon built a small house to reside. With a quiet life filled with enough food and fresh water to keep him content, Blackstone settled into blissful tranquility.

Such happiness was not to last. In 1630, a small party of Puritans who had left England settled upon the Shawmut shore. Desperate for religious freedom and hoping to find good land with fresh water, the Puritans stumbled upon the Shawmut peninsula. They attempted to establish a colony, but found poor water in the region they settled. Blackstone encountered the visitors, took pity on the people, and shared his land with them. The Puritans took to the land and soon more and more Puritans moved into the area.

Within a few years, Blackstone's former enclave of solitude became the center of a burgeoning Puritan colony. When the Puritans officially took over the region, they named the land Boston in honor of the old English city and established a common in the vicinity of Blackstone's home.

Blackstone eventually felt closed in and left for the seclusion of woods to the west.

The Puritans eventually used Blackstone's land to establish grazing fields for their cattle, sheep, and other animals. In time, a city sprung around this land. From these humble beginnings, one of the oldest and most famous commons in America was established — Boston Common.

Today, Boston Common is a vibrant attraction amid the hub of Massachusetts. Complete with trees, walkways, open land, and an abundance of landmarks, the Common is the epitome of all that is Boston. Monuments throughout the Common point to famous Bostonians and historical events that have occurred amid these green pastures and have shared in Beantown's indomitable spirit. And, for those who visit, you can even find a marker, on a building across from the Common, to show the original location of Blackstone's house.

The Mystery

However the history of the Common and the spirit that surrounds it also have a dark side. The Puritans hoped to establish a colony founded on religion that could be admired by the entire world. As the Puritan's established their rule-bound government in Boston, outlawing such things as Christmas and dancing, they also created a testament to all that decadence could bring – a hanging tree. Where else did they put it, but on what is now Boston Common.

No one is quite certain where the old hanging tree on Boston Common is. Most sources from the time suggest it was a large elm tree on the western side of the common that was eventually replaced in 1769 by a gallows. Yet, it is thought to have been active during the first 150 years of Boston.

According to history, the hangman's noose was frequented by many people during the age of the Puritans. Two supposed witches,

Quakers, and those who violated the laws of Boston were subject to the noose. Perhaps no victim was quite so renown as Mary Dyer.

Mary Dyer was a Quaker woman who lived in Rhode Island, a colony formed by Roger Williams who had been banished by the Puritans for his religious beliefs. In the mid 1600s, she visited Boston several times, hoping to diminish the suffering of fellow Quakers who were subjected to Puritans' laws. Dyer went against the Puritan protocol of the day and preached the values and beliefs of Quaker religion to the people of Boston.

This bothered the Puritans immensely. They threatened to hang Dyer if she did not stop her evangelism. In October 1659, after two warnings, the Puritan leaders finally arrested her and a local judge sentenced her to hang along with two other men who had practiced their own religious beliefs.

According to Meg Beste, in the article "Boston's Haunted," on the appointed day of hanging, as the two other men were hanged, Dyer received a last minute reprieve from the governor. At the request of Dyer's son, the governor commuted the sentence and Dyer left the colony with her son, returning home to Rhode Island. However, her voyage home was short-lived. Inspired by her need to evangelize, she returned to the colony soon after and began preaching. When she was caught, tried, and convicted again, the judge attempted to make a bargain with her, perhaps saying something like, "leave Boston forever and the hangman's sentence will be reduced."

Critical of Puritan rule, Dyer did not accept the offer. The judge sentenced her to hang. The following day, the sentence was carried out.

Dyer's death on the hanging tree was one of many hangings that were carried out from the 1600s until 1817, when the gallows were disassembled. While many a life was taken by the noose, not all of those people who died may have left the Common.

Rumors persist to this day that many victims of the gallows still haunt the Common. Exactly who these people are is uncertain. People have spotted images of the victims hanging from trees or wandering near the area where the Central Burying Ground is kept (more on that later). Some witnesses even believe that Mary Dyer herself has materialized at times. A woman wearing a Puritan dress, sometimes weeping, has been spotted walking in the Common.

However, the hangman's victims are not the only spirits that inhabit the sprawling grass of Boston Common. In a section by the Arlington Street entrance lies a fountain with an angel carved on it. Many people resting near this fountain have reported seeing two women, garbed in nineteenth century clothing, walking in a hurry. Their clothing looks similar to that of a Victorian age re-enactor, in a style that had long since passed when the gallows were abolished. Exactly who these women are remains unknown. They do look dressed in their Sunday best and appear to be heading towards a theatre of some sort. They look happy, appear to be talking, and are sometimes seen walking arm and arm. They enjoy their walks and will smile at people they pass. Yet, they do something strange if people try to speak to them or approach — they disappear.

Attempts to determine who these women are have turned up nothing. Locals believe the women may have died in an accident, perhaps struck by a passing vehicle or even a streetcar, at the turn of the twentieth century.

Unusual sightings of these women have persisted to this day.

So the next time you happen to walk through Boston Common, keep a sharp eye open. Not only will you see monuments of the past, but you might just see a little bit of the past as well.

This statue of Mary Dyer is located near the Massachusetts State House. Dyer, who was hanged on the nearby Boston Common, is believed to haunt the famous Common ground.

Charlesgate Hotel

The Story of the
Creepiest Hotel in Town...

The History

I n 1891, the Charlesgate Hotel became a fixture of Boston. Located in what is now the prestigious Back Bay section of the city, the hotel was built by John Pickering Putnam to cater to those who wanted to enjoy the best in American culture. Historians suggest that Putnam may have been motivated by a strong sense of nationalism and his hotel became a gathering place of the wealthy during the "gilded age" that ruled the early twentieth century of the United States.

However, as soon as a federal income tax was established, the gilded age began a slow decline. So, did the hotel. With wealthy patrons no longer able to spend "fun money" on such posh frivolities, the hotel's success slowly dwindled.

In 1920, the hotel became a private residence until the 1940s when Boston University purchased the hotel to establish dorm rooms. Speculation persists that the private residence may have been popular during prohibition, perhaps catering to bootlegging, before it was sold to the college.

When Boston University took over the building, officials renovated the former hotel for student use. The creation of the dormitories – and more than likely the previous use of the building as a private residence – altered the original structure tremendously, often hiding or altering the creative touches of Putnam's design. Rooms and décor changed and it also appeared other rooms were added and later boarded up.

Boston University used the former hotel for dorms until the 1970s, when Emerson College began to use it. Emerson College eventually moved students to other buildings and the former Charlesgate remained abandoned until the 1990s. Originally slated to be demolished in the 1990s, the hotel was rescued from the wrecking ball. The former hotel was renovated to make way for condominiums and now serves as a private residence in Back Bay.

It is important to note that the hotel also has a legacy of other uses that are not so easy to corroborate. During different time periods, the hotel has been thought to be used as a haven for criminals, drug addicts, people who needed shelter from the streets, and a house of ill repute. While it is hard to find proof that the hotel served any of these purposes, local lore suggests that the mysterious past of this building might have helped bring a variety of spirits here as well.

The Mystery

The Charlesgate Hotel has had a sordid history that is often hard to decipher. A mixture of fact and fiction blurs together to make Charlesgate one of Boston's truly amazing haunts.

According to legend, the hotel once featured a horse stable on the first floor. Two of the horses that lived in these stables supposedly died there. Yet, the spirits of these two horses remain to this day, a remnant of the hotel's past glory. Paranormal investigators reportedly videotaped the horses on a trip to the building.

However, horses are just one of the alleged haunts of this hotel turned dorm hall. As with most of Boston's colleges, a variety of ghost stories were passed down from generation to generation, speaking to tragedies that occurred within the dorm walls. Some sources say that a young student hung himself in one of the rooms. His lingering spirit is said to lurk about the premises. Similarly, the presence of a girl who hung herself in one of the dorm rooms was also thought to be felt by residents who lived in her former room. Another tale told about the former dorm suggests that one person, perhaps a female student, was crushed by a malfunctioning elevator or fell to her death when she stepped into an elevator shaft and plunged more than sixty feet. Her spirit, too, is said to roam the old halls of the Charlesgate and the elevator itself was eventually boarded up for more than fifty years. And, still another ghostly tale involves the spirit of a man that was said to hover over the beds of students. The ghost once scared a student so much that the room was closed as living quarters.

A variety of other unknown spirits were also said to haunt the hotel. These spirits range from an elderly man with a beard, a ship captain who liked to scare female students, and several other people who appear to have died from drug overdoses. There's also the spirit of a young girl who was shot to death, and the ghosts of women dressed in flapper clothing — sometimes seen without a head. Shapes of strange animals have been seen patrolling the corridors as well.

The Charlesgate Hotel has earned an almost Hollywood-like reputation for hosting so many ghosts. To this day, accounts of students who claimed the have encounters with the paranormal can be found on websites, magazines, and books. Some even have claimed to conjure spirits in their rooms quite easily, only to have difficulty making them disappear.

Whatever — or whoever — is at the Charlesgate seems to have been tempered in recent years. Few ghost sightings are now reported at the former hotel. Perhaps the spirits of old have finally decided to check in some where else.

The Hampshire House

Where Every Ghost Knows Your Name...

The History

During the 1980s, NBC launched a highly successful sitcom known as Cheers. As loyal fans know, the fictitious bar was set in Boston and proved to be a popular watering hole to residents in the region. And, as fans probably know, the bar itself was inspired by a real bar called The Bull and Finch Pub, located in - you guessed it - Boston.

While the friendly English-style pub provides a cozy confines for visitors to the area, it does have a unique history all its own. The pub is located in a building that originally served as a private residence. Built in 1910 for the family of Judge Bayard Thayer, his wife Susan, and their children, the house was the brainchild of architect Ogden Codman. The Thayers no doubt enjoyed their home opposite Boston Common for sometime until they sold it in the mid 1940s.

The mansion, located in the Beacon Hill section of Boston, was then transformed into a luxury hotel called the Hampshire House. It remained a hotel until 1969, when Jack Veasy and Tom Kershaw purchased the building. There they established a restaurant bearing the hotel's namesake, The Hampshire House, as well as the legendary Bull and Finch Pub, which they established in the basement of the building.

The pub has remained a popular spot in Boston. In 1981, during a visit to Beantown, Cheers' creators Glenn and Mary Ann Charles stumbled upon the bar and found that it would serve as a perfect backdrop for a sitcom they were developing. History was soon born.

The Bull and Finch still exists and serves many customers each day. A second bar was established in Fanueuil Hall, replicating the Boston bar popularized on the sitcom. That bar is known as Cheers.

The Mystery

As with all good Boston landmarks, what would a point of interest be without a grand story. The Bull and Finch is no exception.

Although details surrounding the tale are sketchy, it appears that the days the Thayer family spent in their mansion may not have always been rosy. According to local lore, the Thayers had twin daughters. While one of the girls appears to have lived a happy life, the other daughter apparently suffered from some type of emotional disability. During one of her bouts, she reportedly tied a noose using bed sheets and hanged herself from a large spiral staircase in the house. Rumors have surfaced as to what turmoil may have caused this young girl to commit suicide, but no one truly knows the reason.

As time went on, and though the Thayers moved from the house, the young girl's spirit lingered on. Several people who have visited the former Hampshire House have reported encountering the spirit of the girl. Although these reports are sporadic, the girl appears to be about thirteen years old and very melancholy. She acts reclusive and rarely ventures out when patrons are in the pub. While the ghost does not frequent the bar, she does, occasionally, visit the section of the building that contains the former Hampshire House restaurant. Usually, when active, she is found on the third floor.

Whether or not this spirit is the daughter of the Thayer family remains unknown. However, one thing is for sure… the former Hampshire House might be a place where at least one ghost knows your name.

Huntington Theater

The Ghost Must Go On...

The History

Huntington Theater is run by Boston University for students in the theater arts program. The theater was originally built in the 1920s, as the brainchild of Henry Jewett, a well-known actor and director of his day, who had staged many productions throughout Boston. Jewett wanted a permanent home for his group and designed the playhouse to be a tax-exempt theater for this purpose. Doors to the theater first opened in 1925 as the Henry Jewett Players took to the stage. The theater's location near Symphony Hall and the old Opera House made it a vital part of the artistic scene in Boston. Local residents, including Calvin Coolidge, frequented the theater.

The theater remained popular until the 1930s, when Jewett's troupe disbanded and movies swept the country. Jewett died the same year. The theater began showing movies throughout the 1930s and 1940s under the name Esquire Theater, while occasionally offering a stage production.

In 1953, Boston University purchased the theater and eventually began using it for its intended purpose. For more than thirty years, the university's School of Theater Arts has been performing on the stage of Jewett's once proud theater. Numerous quality productions are staged throughout the year, providing the city, and the college, a chance to share great talent.

The Mystery

The Huntington Theater is not just home to university actors. Other, more ghostly beings have taken up residence there as well. In the book *Ghosts of Boston Town*, author Holly Nadler mentions that the theater is the site of several hauntings, most likely by ghosts that are still enchanted with the stage.

According to eyewitnesses, one of the ghosts often spotted in the building is that of a lady dressed in white clothing. Presumed to be an old stage-hand or perhaps a costume designer, the woman is typically spotted during dress rehearsals. She attends these practices, perhaps casting a critical eye on the sets and costumes, or reminiscing about performances of gone by years, comparing them to the more modern plays appearing on stage.

Another ghost that is said to make a cameo is that of a man who keeps watch over the actors as a shepherd would a flock. The ghost occasionally arrives during the afternoon and can be seen patrolling the halls. The man lurks about as if searching for any unforeseen danger. According to performers, the ghost is always associated with positive energy and is usually viewed as a good luck charm, indicating that an upcoming performance is sure to go well.

Many stories have surfaced about the identity of this ghost. Some people suggest that it might be an early member of Hewitt's troupe who killed himself when his wife left him. Other people suggest the ghost might belong to one of a number of theater patrons of the 1930s who fought hard to maintain the theatrical vitality of the theater in the midst of declining interest. Whoever the ghost is, there is no doubt in the minds of some people that more than actors float about the stage of Boston's old Huntington Theater.

Majestic Theater

The Ghosts of the Stage...

The History

In 1903, construction on the renown Majestic Theater was completed in Boston, Massachusetts. The second oldest theater in Boston's Theater District, it was designed by John Galen Howard and commissioned by Eben Dyer Jordan, the son of the founder of a former Boston-based store chain, Jordan Marsh. The theater was a combination of classic styles that helped set the bar for theaters of the day. It utilized old charm with the latest inventions of the time – light bulbs – to show off the true glory of the stage. The resulting experience combined theater and fine architecture, complete with stained glass windows, columns, and arches, to form this impressive building.

The Majestic Theater was first built to house opera and theatrical productions. However, it has served a variety of purposes during the past one hundred years. In the 1920s, the Shubert Organization managed the theater and used the space to stage Vaudeville acts. In the 1950s, the Majestic Theater was converted into a movie theater, with much of the fine art and architecture hidden from view during those remodeling efforts.

In 1983, Emerson College, a Boston institution known for a commitment to theater, arts, and communication, purchased the theater. They eventually revitalized the theater, transforming it from a Saxon (better known as Sack) Cinema to a state of the art theater facility. Although the restoration took nearly twenty years to complete, new ventilation, new accessibility routes, new stages, and new actor facilities turned the early twentieth century landmark into a twenty-first century triumph. The Cutler Majestic Theater, as it is now called, is home to a variety of arts organizations that perform on stage.

The Mystery

Majestic Theater has maintained a beloved spot in the hearts of Bostonians for centuries. The warm memories of performances staged remind people of the spirits of past actors and actresses who graced the stage.

However, these memories are not the only spirits that might ply the walls, rows, and aisles of the 1,200-seat theater. Popular legends have it that a variety of specters call this place home. The most simple of these legends involve stories of eerie sounds and strange cries that have been reported by visitors. Many students who have attended Emerson College and have spent time working in the theater report sensing unearthly and eerie feelings. Students and visitors suggest that Majestic is haunted by numerous spirits. According to local lore, the spirits of a little girl, a politician, and perhaps even former stage crew and actors have been seen roaming the Majestic.

One of the more popular legends involves a lone ghost that can be occasionally spotted in one of the seats in the theater. According to the stories, the ghost inhabits the seat of a former mayor who died in the theater while watching a performance. Many believe that the mayor reclaims his seat from time to time, coming to take in yet another play before making his own final curtain call.

However, this story pales in comparison to another tale that suggests a row of patrons haunt the facility. As this story goes, two hooligans were climbing in the rafters of the theater during the middle of a performance and, while the performance continued below them, the two hooligans cut the set's lights. The hooligans probably hoped to cause a stir on stage. However, following a more Phantom of the Opera ending, the falling lights caused significant damage. They came crashing down, not on stage as the hooligans may have thought, but onto a row of spectators, killing them in the middle of the play. The ghosts of these theater lovers are believed to frequent the theater, waiting for the next grand performance.

A third rumor involves what is now an unused balcony of the theater. This balcony contains steep seats that, at one point, were used by minority and poor citizens of the city in the early days of the theater. As time has passed, segregation ended, and safety codes have changed, the seats have been deemed hazardous and are unavailable to the general public. However, not everyone has been made aware of that fact. According to the Massachusetts Paranormal Crossroads website, many theater workers report that the balcony is the most haunted hot spot of the theater. The seats, which are extremely heavy and should typically remain in an upright position, often are pushed down when theater workers go to check the section. Dust and dirt that might normally cover the seats of the chairs somehow seemed to be wiped off as if people have been watching a performance. Seats have even moved up and down during shows for no apparent reason. Technicians have reported talking to a man in the balcony, only to report that he disappears seconds later, when they turn around to face him. Other workers claim to have spotted two adults, and a child, dressed in Victorian clothing sitting in this section, awaiting a performance.

The ghostly haunts are not just relegated to the seats. Students who have performed sound duties during plays and rehearsals have also reported mysterious occurrences. At times, the power in the theater remains on, but the sound shuts off for no apparent reason. Typically, this sets off the timing of a performance and can cause general havoc on stage and off. Speculation exists that it's the ghosts causing such mischief and might even be sharing their opinion about the performance. If they don't like the show, they let the players know.

The renovations in the theater seemed to draw out much of the ghostly energy. The spirits appear to approve of the new direction that theater owners are taking. Many workers associated with the theater admit to being frightened by the spirits, but also speak of them as regular entities, trying not to block their views in the balcony and respecting their presence. Most report that the spirits seem to be friendly and want to reconnect to a theater that brought them much joy in the past. And for that reason, the show continues to go on.

Myles Standish Hall

The College of Multiple Ghosts...

The History

Myles Standish Hall is a nine story dormitory named for one of the Pilgrim leaders that arrived in Plymouth in 1620. The hall, located in Kenmore Square, was opened as the Myles Standish Hotel in 1928. Serving a variety of patrons in the late 1920s, 1930s, and 1940s, the hotel attracted a lot of attention during its tenure. Its proximity to Fenway Park, home of the Red Sox, made it particularly popular with baseball players. Babe Ruth, who once played for the Olde Towne Team, used to stay at the hotel whenever the Yankees visited the city, always requesting room 818.

Historians speculate that the hotel also housed a speakeasy during the days of prohibition. Located in the basement or bottom floors of the building, the bootleg operation probably drew a diverse population. Undoubtedly, some of the visiting baseball players probably imbibed at the hotel after their games. The hotel, though popular, never prospered because of troubles it faced opening during the era of the Depression.

In 1949, Boston University was in need of dorm space, particularly with an influx of students registering at the school under the G.I. Bill. They purchased the hotel and renovated it for students. The University has housed many students in the building since that time, and it has gained its own claim to fame at the university.

The Mystery

The hall is home to some rather unusual stories and is often considered one of the most haunted buildings on the sprawling campus of Boston University. According to Julianne Klimetz in *The Daily Free Press*, the dormitory is just one of several haunted dorms at the university... and a few ghosts supposedly permeate the building.

Klimetz interviewed students who have reported ghostly goings-on. Two students claimed that a ghost – or some type of supernatural phenomenon – visited their room, moving furniture and opening drawers in a chest, while they were out one evening.

While there is not a lot of proof of who these ghosts might be, the stories told about the dorm might help pinpoint a few of the suspects. Babe Ruth was particularly fond of the building and is believed to have spent a lot of time there. Residents of the dorm have claimed that Babe Ruth has wandered down the hall or passed through the walls.

Other students claim that the ghost of the building may belong to the infamous Boston Strangler. In the 1960s, the Strangler was known for murdering women throughout the city. One of his last victims resided in the building. Students claim that the murderer himself, or even one of his victims, haunts the dorm.

Then, there is also the idea that the inspiration for a famous literary figure also haunts the building. As Klimetz explains in her article, the dormitory was supposedly the home of playwright Arthur Miller's uncle. Miller based the character of Willy Loman in *Death of a Salesman* on his uncle who took his life in the building. There are some students who avoid the ninth floor – where this suicide reportedly happened – just for that reason.

Perhaps the most interesting ghost story of all takes us back to the days of the first settlers to New England – the Pilgrims. According to Patrick Day of *The Daily Free Press*, there are some students who claim the namesake for the building, none other than the Pilgrim leader himself, Myles Standish, wanders the hall. Occasionally he has appeared in a dining room, checking out the latest dish, or meandering down the hallways of the dorm. What exactly might draw Standish to the hall is unknown. After all, he lived two centuries before Boston University was even established. Maybe he is simply curious to learn about the building that bears his name.

Of course, not all students believe in the ghostly hauntings of Myles Standish Hall. These non-believers suggest that all of the strange occurrences are a result of a building that is decades old.

So who is right? No one knows. But, chances are there is probably a great story behind the mysteries of Myles Standish Hall. It is just waiting to be discovered…or seen.

Omni Parker House

Where Ghosts Check in…
Permanently?

The History

In the heart of Boston resides a charming hotel that has a special spot in American history. Called the Omni Parker house, the hotel is the oldest continuously operating hotel in the United States. But that is only a small portion of its celebrated history. The entire story of the hotel, from its early foundations to its present day status as a glorious reminder of the golden age of hotels, is an amazing tale.

The founder of the hotel was a man named Harvey Parker, who arrived on the streets of Boston in 1825 with a dollar to his name. He quickly got a job caring for cattle and horses that paid a meager $104 a year. Once settled, he eventually became a coach driver for a wealthy woman from nearby Watertown.

According to authors Mary Beth Sammons and Robert Edwards, Parker left the job in 1832 and had earned enough money to purchase a small restaurant, and rename it Parker's. By 1854, Parker's was a local hot spot, frequented by politicians, attorneys, and entrepreneurs of the area. Parker realized the restaurant was just the beginning of his success and decided to go onto bigger things – opening an exclusive hotel to cater to Bostonians and those who wished to visit the city.

In the spring of 1854, Parker chose the site of a large boarding house for his endeavor – the site of a building called the Mico Mansion. He had the mansion demolished and built a five-story hotel in its place. The hotel featured brick, stone, and marble construction. Rich ornamentation decorated the halls and lobby and the hotel itself became a fashion statement. In 1855, the Omni Parker House opened to the public. It became an instant hit, attracting many celebrities of that age…and a lot more. Nathaniel Hawthorne, Charles Dickens, and even Henry Wadsworth Longfellow checked into the hotel. Over the years, other well-known Americans have patronized the hotel, from famous presidents such as Ulysses Grant and Franklin Delano Roosevelt, to baseball legend Babe Ruth. The hotel was even host to the top actors of its day, such as Sarah Bernhardt, Edwin Booth, Judy Garland, and Adam West.

The hotel holds other fascinating claims to fame. It is the prestigious home to two of America's most favorite foods. The Parker House roll, beloved throughout the world, first appeared in the stoves of the acclaimed hotel. And, the equally loved Boston Cream Pie was also an invention of the Omni Parker House kitchen. The word scrod, used to describe a small portion of fresh cod, was coined in the hotel. The hotel has become so famous that chefs throughout the world have trained in the kitchen, including chef Emeril Lagasse. And, it has also been home to a variety of famous employees including Ho Chi Minh, who worked as a busboy, and Malcolm X, who was a waiter.

The hotel also hosted an infamous resident in the mid 1800s. John Wilkes Booth, a well-known actor of the day, stayed at the hotel in 1865 for a few days, probably to visit his brother Edwin who was performing in the city. John Wilkes Booth was spotted at a neighborhood shooting range practicing with a pistol before leaving Boston for Washington D.C. At the time, people assumed it was just Booth rehearsing for an upcoming play, but some scholars now believe it was a prelude to his assassination of Abraham Lincoln. Shortly after he left, he shot Lincoln to death.

In 1925, forty-one years after Parker's death, the hotel began showing its age and renovations began. Most of the hotel was torn down, but a small portion remained operational, giving way to a fourteen story grand edition that reopened in 1927. In recent years, the Omni hotel chain has purchased the hotel and preserved the hospitable charm established in the building so many years ago. To this day, the hotel remains a beautiful landmark and a testimony to creativity and hard work in the city of Boston.

The Mystery

Despite the diverse history of the hotel, the 551-room landmark continues to be one of the most popular hot spots in Boston. However, it has also proven to be one of the most haunted. A variety of ghost stories have permeated the lobby, halls, and rooms of Boston's hotel. Lights mysteriously go on and off, elevators move up and down on their own, doors creak open, and footsteps are heard patrolling some rooms. Occasional voices penetrate the air. Even a few spirits, dressed in Victorian styles and haircuts, have been spotted in various parts of the hotel.

Speculation is strong that one of the spirits inhabiting the hotel is Parker himself. He has been spotted by many people, including guests. Parker, it is said, commonly meanders throughout the hotel. Typically, he can be found wandering the halls on the tenth floor, which, ironically, did not exist when he owned the hotel. Often, he disappears shortly after he is seen. In other parts of the hotel, Parker makes himself known in other ways. Workers and patrons go into rooms and find furniture that has been rearranged without any known cause. Some believe that this may be attributed to Parker continuing to leave his mark on the hotel. Construction workers who have renovated the building reported seeing a man that resembled Parker walking through the hotel wearing a hard hat. When the workers pursued the man, he often turned a corner and simply vanished.

Parker may not be the only person who has had a hard time checking out. The third floor of the hotel is a particularly active spot. According to writer Charlyn Keating Chisholm, this floor is believed to be haunted by the ghost of actress Charlotte Cushman. The famed Shakespearean actress of the late nineteenth century was a hotel patron. She died in her third floor room while staying one night in 1876. Some visitors believe you can feel her chilling presence when you enter her former room. One of the elevators makes periodic stops to the third floor without warning, when no buttons are pressed and no guests are riding on it. Perhaps it is the actress returning to her room once again.

The third floor might be the site of some other ghostly figures as well. Room 303 is often said to be the home of a special ghost. The sound of rowdy laughter, the hint of alcohol, even the presence of a spirit suggest that someone still visits the room. Most ghost hunters believe the ghost was a businessman who died in the room, probably of accidental self-inflicted alcohol poisoning. So many guests commented about the eerie presence over the years, and the form of a strange man that would materialize in the room as well as the mysterious odor of alcohol, that the room was eventually converted into a closet.

Another presence that might visit the third floor is thought to be none other than Henry Wadsworth Longfellow. According to popular lore, Longfellow and close friends Charles Dickens (when he stayed in Boston), Henry Thoreau, and Ralph Waldo Emerson met in the hotel to discuss stories and events of the day. Their group, called "The Saturday Club," enjoyed the hotel. Longfellow seemed to be partial to one room that he always requested on the third floor. It is believed that he, too, might return to his favorite room every now and then when that elevator stops at the third floor.

Perhaps Longfellow has a reason to visit. He may not be the only member of the Saturday Club to still call the Omni Parker house a transcendent home. Another member of the club purchased a large mirror and gifted it to the hotel. The mirror has moved about the hotel – under the power of employees – over the years. However, many people who look in the mirror claim to see an image looking back at them. Though fuzzy, the image clearly looks like a man. Who is this celebrated figure and member of the Saturday Club? You guessed it – none other than the person who penned a tale about three famous holiday ghosts – Charles Dickens himself.

Other ghosts may have made themselves known as well. Visitors to the upper floors have reported glowing lights and orbs floating through the air. Occasionally, water faucets have turned on and off on their own. And, patrons have reported seeing strange shadows throughout the building.

So, the next time you pass by the Omni Parker House, take a careful look. You might just see someone famous checking in… yet again.

Shelton Hall

The Pulitzer Prize Winning Ghost...

The History

Shelton Hall is a nine-story dormitory owned and operated by Boston University. The hall has a nebulous history. It was originally built as one of the first Sheraton Hotels in 1923 (in fact, some sources claim it is the first Sheraton Hotel and others suggest that it may have opened in the late 1800s). The hotel contained apartment style rooms and was used by tourists and local residents alike, catering to many of the social elite of the day.

The hotel stood out as a beautiful example of early twentieth century architecture. The ornate decoration inside the hotel made it a lavish retreat. The top floor of the building had a scenic view of the Charles River and the Boston skyline. In the early 1900s, the hotel included a small dance hall and stage that is believed to be the sight of parties held by the best and brightest of Boston.

In 1950, the hotel was sold to the Sonnabend family that renamed it the Hotel Shelton. Local rumor has it that the family chose a new name that began with S to cut down on the amount of monogram changes that needed to be made throughout the hotel. The family, who eventually started the Sonesta chain of hotels, ran the Hotel Shelton for four years, and then sold it to Boston University.

When Boston University purchased the hotel in 1954, they renamed it Shelton Hall. B.U. turned it into a dorm and still uses the residence to house several hundred students, mostly upperclassmen. Students often consider it one of the "dream dorms" to live in. The hall is located near Kenmore Square and students on the eighth floor often can hear Red Sox games during the early fall and late spring.

During its days as a hotel, a variety of notables took up residence there. Ted Williams, the slugger for the Boston Red Sox, lived in the hotel for many years. In the 1930s, Jeanette MacDonald, a legendary opera singer of the day, also called the hotel home. Perhaps the most famous resident was Pulitzer and Nobel prize winning playwright Eugene O'Neill, who moved into the hotel with his wife, Carlotta, when she developed a mental illness that caused her to experience hallucinations. He stayed at the hotel for several years in the 1950s, living there with his wife, while a doctor who specialized in mental illness lived down the hall, ready to lend a hand at a moment's notice. O'Neill routinely stayed in room 401 in a section of the hall now dubbed Writer's Corridor.

O'Neill's life deteriorated while he stayed in the hotel. His health failed. He developed Parkinson's disease, suffered from stomach problems, and contracted tuberculosis while staying in the hotel. He also developed bouts of frustration. Within a year of staying in the hotel, O'Neill stopped writing altogether, destroying any copies of unfinished works he had started.

On November 27, 1953, O'Neill reached the end of his career. Drinking numerous shots of whiskey at night, O'Neill apparently died of alcohol poisoning. He passed into the night and into the halls of literary greats. An amazing writer had been lost to the world.

The Mystery

O'Neill's final day in life may not have been his last. Upon his death, Carlotta stayed in room 401 and reported that her husband often visited her from beyond the grave. She mentioned that they engaged in conversation frequently. Many skeptics doubted Carlotta's theory, assuming that the return of her husband was one of her hallucinations. However, there have been numerous accounts to validate Carlotta's belief that her husband, indeed, may never have abandoned the final scene of his life.

After Carlotta left and the property was turned over to Boston University, students began to notice odd occurrences in Shelton Hall. Over the years, reports of strange events have persisted from those who lived on the fourth floor and in room 401, which students still use. Most are attributed to O'Neill's spirit.

In *Ghosts of Boston*, writers Joseph Mont and Marcia Weaver explain that there are many signs in Shelton Hall associated with O'Neill's ghost. Often, a sure sign of O'Neill's arrival is heralded by a banging noise that permeates room 401 and the hall on the fourth floor. Strange voices have been heard in the night, sometimes whispering the names of residents who live in the building. Lights on the floor and in the room occasionally dim or flicker, perhaps the result of a playwright who still has a lot of ambition. Toilets flush in some rooms on the floor when no one is in the bathroom. Even windows seem to be impervious to the spirits on the fourth floor. Occasionally, window shades rock or move, as if being pushed despite the fact that there is no one near the windows and no breeze blowing into the room.

According to Brian Fitzgerald in a 1999 edition of B. U. Bridge, residents have also reported strange knocks at their doors. When the doors are answered, inevitably no one is there. Knocks also echo off the walls of vacant rooms. Students have also reported shadowy figures running through the hall, after most students have left for vacation. Some residents have suggested that to merely open a copy of his plays such as *The Ice Man Cometh* in room 401, will cause O'Neill to make his presence known. He will cause lights to flicker or window shades to shift.

Even when room 401 is abandoned and residents are gone, the presence long attributed to O'Neill makes itself known. The windows in room 401 often open on their own for no apparent reason when no one is staying in the room. Strange noises have also been heard by people staying in the room below 401, particularly when 401 is abandoned.

While Eugene O'Neill may be the most celebrated ghost to haunt the floors of Shelton, there are many other specters that have been seen spending time in the dormitory as well. On the bottom floor of the hall is an old hallway, custodian's room, and a laundry room. The hallway is filled with many alcoves that resemble small closets and doorways that were used at some time in the past. For residents of the dorm who wander the hallway to do laundry, these alcoves may sometimes present a formidable fright.

On occasion, residents have reported hearing strange noises and groans penetrating the stale air of these alcoves. The sounds resemble the call of animals or the low bay of an angry dog. However, despite searching, residents who have heard the strange sounds report that they have never found a source for the eerie noise. Yet, just the presence of the sounds has led some residents to avoid that section of the hall at all costs.

Although several residents have reported strange sightings in the hall over the years, there are many who have not had an encounter with any restless spirits, which leads to the speculation that the rumors of ghosts is just a figment of many imaginations. Exactly who or what is residing in Shelton Hall remains to be seen. But, just perhaps, it is O'Neill, continuing to inspire stories long after he left this world.

Part Two:

Two if by Sea

Boston may have been a beacon on a hill, but it cut its teeth by the sea. With the waters surrounding Boston rich in fish and stocked with whales, the first settlers took immediately to the sea. Stocks of fish and later whale oil were gleaned from these briny Atlantic waters. As times changed and Boston became a more industrialized city, the Boston ports became a mecca of trade. To this day, Boston waterways are still popular, catering to fisherman, tourists, and businesses alike.

While Boston's waterways have been home to a flurry of activity, they have also been home to an array of local lore. Tales of shipwrecks, pirates, lighthouses, battles, and small disasters at sea are hallmarks of these legends around Boston. The famed Boston Harbor islands alone are a virtual treasure trove of ghostly tales.

There is little doubt, then, that some of Boston's haunted history has been swept up with the tides. Many ghost stories have been told about the chilly Atlantic waters that brush up against the city. Come and see why Boston's waterways are among America's most haunted.

The view from Lewis Wharf in Boston. It was once a huge center of trade. Many people now claim that the wharf is haunted.

Apple Island

Ghostly Lovers...

The History

Apple Island is the name of a small island found off the coast of East Boston. Although diminutive in size, it certainly earned a large reputation. Because of sandbars and flat patches of land in and around the isle, it was considered one of the most dangerous spots in the harbor. It has since become one of the most forgotten spots.

Apple Island first came to the attention of Bostonians in the late seventeenth century and early eighteenth century. The island was owned by a man named Thomas Hutchinson, whose son, by the same name, later served as royal governor of Massachusetts prior to the Revolutionary War. The Hutchinsons owned the island until 1724, when it began to pass through the hands of several owners.

In 1760, James Mortimer purchased the island and built a large house on it. The island became a small farm, and Mortimer raised various kinds of crops and livestock on it. The house remained in the Mortimer family during the late 1700s. The American army probably visited the island during the Revolutionary War, commandeering the livestock for their own purposes. The island, though still owned by the Mortimer family following the Revolution, was abandoned by its heirs.

By the early 1800s, no one lived on the island, and it became a shell of its former self. In 1814, William Marsh, a boat aficionado from the mainland, visited the island. He had heard about the Mortimer homestead and decided to see if it still stood. Upon finding the old home, he realized that it was an ideal place to stay, particularly during the robust autumn gales that plagued the harbor. He frequented the house during his ventures in the harbor and eventually claimed it as his home later that year. Not to be confused with a squatter, Marsh searched for the owners of the house and eventually purchased it in 1830. During the time that Marsh lived as a tenant on the land, the U.S. military developed plans to build a fort on the island. But, they eventually scrapped the plan and fortified other islands.

In 1867, the island was sold to the city of Boston for nearly $4,000. In the latter part of the 1800s, Apple Island became home to a mixture of residents including Portuguese immigrants, people who ran illegal boxing matches, and private owners who built seasonal cottages on the island. The island and the cottages became a popular tourist escape in the early twentieth century, until a group of vandals set fire to the cozy seasonal homes. Following the vandalism, the island was deserted.

In 1945, the idyllic island met its destiny. As part of Boston's efforts to grow, the now desolate Apple Island became incorporated into a plan to expand Boston's airport. Eventually, Apple Island was connected to the mainland with fill and the once tranquil isle became part of the facility known as Logan Airport. There it remains to this day, a footnote in history, touched by people all around the world.

The Mystery

Apple Island always had an air of mystery around it. From a long list of owners to unusual characters who set up shop on the isle, Apple Island had seen it all. And, it is very likely that it saw the birth of at least one good ghost story.

Author Edward Rowe Snow was one of several people who have suggested the island may have been haunted by star-crossed lovers. In the book *The Islands of Boston Harbor*, Snow narrates a tale of sadness that blossomed into legend.

The tale begins sometime in the late eighteenth century or early nineteenth century, when a young socialite of Boston disappeared without a trace. Because she was the daughter of the local governor, the city put out a tremendous effort to find her. After two weeks of searching and no leads, her body washed up on the shore of Apple Island.

While the death may have been an accident, or just a cruel twist of fate, many Bostonians suspected foul play. At the time, Apple Island was a hideout for a small group of ruffians. Many citizens of Boston suspected that this group of outlaws had something to do with the socialite's sudden disappearance and death. So, too, did her boyfriend.

Incensed by the thought that the group may have murdered his true love, the boyfriend was bent on revenge. He decided to sail to Apple Island and infiltrate the group. He hoped to learn the truth behind the disappearance and pay them back in his own way. For weeks, no one heard from the boyfriend. It appeared that he had blended in with the group. But, actually something more horrific probably occurred because, weeks later, a local fisherman was passing by the island. He gazed up and he saw the body of a man dangling from a nearby tree. Knowing about the dangerous band of men that roamed the island, the fisherman pulled away from the isle and alerted city officials about the hanging corpse. Officials returned the next day to claim the body and put an end to the group once and for all. While they were able to recover of the body of the man – and identify him as the boyfriend – they were unable to locate the outlaws. They seemed to have vanished into thin air.

However, as with all good ghost stories, the tale did not end there. Visitors to the island in the 1800s up until the early 1900s reported strange sightings of a man and a woman roaming the beach or resting beneath a tree, long after people had abandoned the island. They seemed to be enjoying their company, though apparently were not of this earth. Who exactly were they? Most visitors described them similarly to the star-crossed lovers who had died many years before.

Times have changed and the island no longer exists like it once did. And, sightings of the lovers are no longer reported. However, it is still possible that somewhere on the old Apple Island, are two lovers who finally were reunited, forever, in the afterlife.

Long Wharf in Boston once teemed with local business. It is now home to tourists, boaters, and a few local spirits.

Boston Light

The Haunted Light of Boston...

The History

In the early years of Boston, ships by the dozen came to the city as part of the Great Migration of people from Europe. This migration resulted in a boon in the population of the colonies. Yet, it also caused a pressing need for water safety, as captains and crew alike soon found that the waters around Boston could prove quite treacherous.

As a result of the dangerous shipping lanes, several lighthouses have been established in Boston. The first beacons on the coast were nothing more than lanterns placed on poles guiding ships at sea. By the beginning of the eighteenth century, Bostonians began suggesting the need for lighthouses to be built in the city. In 1713, Boston businessman John George answered the call. Moonlighting as a selectman, he presented the idea of constructing the first true lighthouse for the city. George's proposition was met with open arms and resulted in the establishment of the Boston Light Bill, passed in July 1715.

Under this bill, the city's first manned lighthouse was built on what was then called Beacon Island, but is now known as Little Brewster Island. Funded by a tax paid on ships entering the harbor, and made of stone that stretched more than two stories into the sky, construction lasted about a year and the beacon opened for operation on September 14, 1716.

This first lighthouse was originally manned by George Worthylake, who lived on nearby Great Brewster Island. Worthylake had spent many years around the harbor, growing up on George's Island and tending to crops on Lovell's Island. His trip to the lighthouse was actually quite short – Great Brewster and Little Brewster islands were attached by a narrow sandbar, which often disappeared during high tide or storms.

Worthylake earned fifty pounds a year as the lightkeeper. He tended to the light with the help of his wife, Ann, daughters, Ruth and Ann, and a slave named Shadwell. This, along with a flock of sheep, helped keep the Worthylake family busy.

Worthylake operated the lighthouse capably until tragedy struck on November 3, 1718. Worthylake, his wife, and daughter Ruth went to Boston to collect his pay. This was a typical trip they frequently made. However, as they prepared to leave, a thin fog interspersed with a light rain spread throughout the harbor. According to local lore, it appears the Worthylakes decided to cancel the trip. However, because young Ruth enjoyed the trips, she became disappointed at the sudden change of plans. So, the Worthylakes decided to wait and see if the weather improved. When the conditions modified slightly, the Worthylakes made their way to Boston.

Exactly what happened next is subject to conjecture. Some scholars believe the Worthylakes went to Boston, collected George's pay, and prepared to return to the lighthouse. They sailed out on a small boat and met Shadwell, who was waiting for them in a small canoe, ready to take the Worthylakes and a family friend named John Edge to Little Brewster Island where Ann and a friend were waiting.

As the canoe made its way toward shore, a sudden wave struck. Overloaded with cargo and passengers, the canoe tipped, with the passengers and contents spilling into the cool Atlantic waters. Young Ann watched in horror as all five people drowned in the perilous waters off the shore of the island.

Other historians offer a different perspective of the event. This story unfolds as the Worthylakes and Shadwell enter a small boat and begin rowing toward Boston. On their way toward the city, the weather worsened as a thick fog swallowed the boat. Somewhere, in the midst of Boston Harbor, the boat disappeared. The Worthlyakes and Shadwell were never heard from again. Their ship washed ashore several months later, but their bodies were never found.

Exactly which story is true is known only to history – though it does appear that the Worthylakes' bodies were recovered. However, the disappearance of the Worthylakes had an impact on the city. The tragedy was even commemorated by a young Benjamin Franklin, a twelve-year old lad, who wrote a poem about the drowning at his brother's request. Called "The Lighthouse Tragedy," Franklin showed his early penchant for journalism by selling the poem in the streets of Boston.

Ship captain Robert Saunders followed the Worthylakes as the second lighthouse keeper. Only a few days into his tenure, he also drowned at sea. While the job of lighthouse keeper at Boston Light initially seemed a precarious profession, the third lighthouse keeper, and subsequent keepers, were able to establish the lighthouse as a sturdy and important beacon in the Boston Harbor island chain, while having their own unique adventures. During the history of the lighthouse, stories of rum manufacturing, illegal cigar making, treasure hunting, and shellfish harvesting have been attributed to the keepers who tended the light.

Despite the strange host of events at the lighthouse over the past three centuries, the beacon has evolved into an integral landmark of the city. The first fog horn used in America – a cannon – was placed used at the lighthouse in 1719. The site was also the place of several skirmishes during the Revolutionary War as British soldiers and Patriots volleyed for control of the light until the British destroyed it in July 1776. The lighthouse was rebuilt and opened in 1783 under orders of then Massachusetts' governor John Hancock. Over the years, the lighthouse has been rebuilt, reconstructed, and modified. The lighthouse eventually became property of the United States Coast Guard, which maintains the light to this day.

The Mystery

There is little doubt about the historical significance of America's first lighthouse, which still plays a vital role today in the shipping lanes of Massachusetts. Although nearly three hundred years of history have played itself out on the island, not all of its hallowed past has drifted on to the annals of history. In fact, several hints of the past have periodically resurfaced, reminding Bostonians of the unique and tragic past of this landmark, and making it one of America's most haunted lighthouses.

Some of the most amazing encounters involve the early occupants of the lighthouse. In the article "The Darker Side of Boston Harbor's Lighthouses," author Jeremy D'Entremont explains that the largest flurry of activity occurred in 1947, when Mazie Anderson, the wife of Coast Guard lighthouse keeper Russell Anderson, became involved with many encounters of a supernatural kind. According to Mazie, her awareness of a presence on the island first occurred when she was walking along the shore of Little Brewster Island. As the waves gently lapped the beach during one of her strolls, she heard footsteps approaching from behind. Because the island had few inhabitants, she was eager to greet the latest visitor. However, she was stunned to turn around and find no one behind her. Later that evening, as she drifted off to sleep, she awoke with a start... feeling an unusual presence in the room, watching her.

Mazie's encounters did not end there. She reported that sometimes she heard strange laughter coming from the boathouse near the beacon. She noted, too, the lighthouse beacon once went on and off by itself, as did the fog signal, with no apparent cause. Another time, she heard a girl's voice crying from the area that contained the fog horn. The voice seemed to be crying the words "Shadwell." At the time, Mazie was unfamiliar with the term, and had no idea that it was the name of the Worthylakes' slave. On another day, as Mazie gazed up at the beacon to determine the cause of the sudden commotion, the figure of a girl appeared near the lens. The figure seemed to be creating a sobbing noise that was followed by unusual laughter coming from the room housing the beacon.

Mazie remembered the strange occurrences for some time. It was only years later, when she learned the tragic history of the lighthouse and its earliest occupants, that she began to put the story together and realize that she may have had a ghostly encounter with the prior tenants. What is even more amazing is that Mazie reported the date that she heard the name Shadwell first emanate from the lips of the ghostly lass. The date was November 1, close to the anniversary of the death of the Worthylakes more than two centuries earlier.

Over the years, lightkeepers and visitors have reported seeing the apparition of a woman in the lighthouse. The woman often looks stoic having little expression. She wanders through the house without acknowledging anyone as she passes. She often enters the living quarters, going in one door and out another.

According to D'etremont, even contemporary lighthouse keepers seem to report the presence of unusual and sometimes unnatural events at the lighthouse. During the 1980s, the Coast Guard keepers at the lighthouse, including Dennis Devers, had strange encounters with unknown forces in the lighthouse. Devers reported a radio in the boathouse would often change from rock stations to classical stations without any warning. Devers also mentioned that he once saw the figure of a man looking out of the lantern house. Because there were few inhabitants of the island, Devers checked out the house only to discover that no one was there.

The appearance of such a ghost is not just relegated to eerie shadows and figures. Reports of mysterious footprints appearing in snow have also occurred. The prints resemble those made by a man's boot. They seem to start from nowhere and go nowhere, as if they evaporated into thin air.

No one is certain about the nature of this phenomenon. To be sure, the island itself has been subject to much tragedy, from the incident with the Worthylakes and Shadwell to the untimely death of Robert Saunders. However, the island has also played host to several known shipwrecks — with the bodies of at least three victims buried on the island. Along with these, the bodies of animals have been also buried, including at least one dog as well as numerous sheep that were stuck on the island when the tide changed. Perhaps it is the ghost of one of these victims or animals that inhabits the island to this day. Whatever it is, no tenure at Boston Light is ever complete without trying to find the strange ghosts that haunt the island.

Castle Island

The Strange Specter of the Creepiest Fort in Town...

The History

Castle Island has been a unique part of the Boston Harbor Island chain. Home to Fort Independence, the island was a strategic point of defense for ships entering and leaving the harbor.

Over the years, hundreds of soldiers called Fort Independence home. In 1827, perhaps its most famous resident took the fort as a temporary home. Newly enlisted in the armed services, this Boston native, who you will get to know later, became fascinated with the fort. This young man enjoyed wandering through the fort during his patrols and delighted in the scenic vistas it had to offer.

One of the objects that caught the young man's fancy was a memorial to a fallen soldier that had been crafted out of stone. The memorial was dedicated to a man named Lieutenant Robert Massie, who had fallen on the spot on Christmas Day ten years earlier.

The soldier became so intrigued that he needed to learn more about Massie. Yet, what he soon learned would trouble him forever.

The Mystery

The mystery of this island begins that day when our young soldier became interested in the fate of the lieutenant who had died on the fort's soil. Perhaps aware that no battle was fought on the shores of Boston at the time of the lieutenant's death, the soldier's curiosity blossomed. Upon speaking with the soldiers at the fort, he learned that Lieutenant Massie's death was truly tragic.

Massie arrived as a recent transplant to the fort in 1817. A 21-year-old officer from Virginia, Massie served a similar position at the fort. His apparent jovial manner and friendliness made him a popular soldier amongst the men. However, his pleasant ways caught the attention of another officer named Captain Green (in some versions of the story, the man's name is Lieutenant Gustavus Drane). Green had a reputation among other soldiers as an aggressive and sometimes abrasive character. For reasons unknown, Green took an immediate dislike to Massie.

On December 24, 1817, the eve of Christmas, most of the soldiers were obliged to stay at the fort on duty. Hoping to pass time during the cold winter day, many of the officers gathered to play cards. In the middle of one of the card games, Green became irate, stood up, and accused Massie of cheating. Green demanded satisfaction and challenged Massie to a duel the following day.

Not one to back down from the challenge, Massie agreed. They awoke on a frigid Christmas Day and met outside the barracks at dawn. Both men chose their weapons – swords. Despite attempts by their seconds to dissuade them from fighting, neither man would back down.

The duel commenced at sunrise and within a matter of moments, Green, an expert swordsmen, had fatally pierced the chest of Massie who was less capable with the blade. Several soldiers who had gathered to watch the fight carried Massie inside their fort, where he died later that day.

The news of Massie's death spread throughout the fort and the men became enraged. They mourned the passing of their friend and felt the twinge of anger toward Green grow with each passing day. The soldiers erected the memorial to Massie in honor of their fallen comrade. Yet, it not only honored him, but further emblazoned their passionate anger toward Green.

As days passed, the men soon learned that Green had supposedly killed six other men in such duels. This incensed them further and soon they plotted a quick revenge. From these embers, a devious scheme unfolded.

One dark night, several of the men gathered with Green. Acting friendly, shielding any hint of aloofness, the men passed the time with Green, serving him wine. Green drank a bit too much and soon fell into their trap. Not aware of what was happening, Green was lifted onto the men's shoulders and carried out of the room and into the bowels of the fort, the basement, which had doubled as a prison and a dungeon in times of need. He was placed into one of these small dungeon rooms.

Once there, Green's intoxication began to wear off. As it did, he began to realize the predicament he was in. The soldiers who had passed the night in fond celebration with him were actually completing a treacherous act. His hands and legs were shackled to iron cuffs cast in stone. And the men…well the men were sealing up the small room up with bricks.

Green shouted to the men and demanded his release. However, his orders were ignored as, slowly, the men patched the wall with the last brick. His demands turned to shouting, but were quickly cloaked as the mortar solidified. Green spent his last days sealed inside the fort in what, no doubt, was a horrific death.

Shortly after Green's death, soldiers stationed at the fort reported seeing a strange vision of a ghost floating in the air over the fort. The ghost was dressed in a military uniform as it hovered over the fort. The appearance of the specter caused several men to desert the post.

Our young soldier stationed at the fort in 1827 took notes on everything he heard regarding the story of Massie, Green, the duel, and the act of revenge. His preoccupation with the events began to arouse suspicion of other soldiers at the barracks, who reported him to his superior officers. The superiors spoke to him regarding the story he had heard, and told him never to repeat a single word of it. At the time, the soldier agreed.

What exactly happened at the fort remained conjecture for many years. Our soldier himself may not have totally believed the story – after all, it would seem odd that no one in the Army would wonder about the disappearance of Captain Green – but undoubtedly he found it an intriguing tale.

However, as time passed and the fort began to enter into a state of disrepair, workmen arrived to begin renovations in 1905. As construction got underway, several of the men began work in the basement of the building, where they stumbled upon a strange area walled in with bricks. Intrigued by the strange barricade – particularly in the dungeon – the men decided to demolish the wall. They tore into the bricks with their tools, only to realize that there were several layers of brick sealing off this room. How peculiar!

After an hour, the men were able to make a small hole into the sealed off room. One man, lantern in tow, ventured inside to find out exactly why the wall was sealed off. Moments later, the reason became clear, as he shouted to his fellow workers that he had found a skeleton.

The men quickly tore down the rest of the wall, unveiling the remains of a skeleton, shackled in chains and wearing a uniform dating from the early nineteenth century. Was it the remains of Captain Green? Or, perhaps, it belonged to someone else. No one knew the identity of the remains, so the soldier was buried in a grave marked "Unknown" in the Castle Island cemetery. Either way, reports of a ghostly apparition dressed in a similar uniform persist to this day.

As for Massie, well, his remains, too, were also excavated. He was moved to three other locations, eventually taking up final residence in the Fort Devens cemetery in Ayer, Massachusetts.

And, what about our soldier who delved into the mystery in the first place back in 1827; the man who told his superior officers that the story would remain theirs forever? Well, he did not ride off into the sunset. He remembered the story and eventually retold it to others—in his own way. Perhaps you have heard his version of the story where events and circumstances have been changed to protect the innocent. For if you have read *The Cask of the Amontillado*, then you are familiar with the story written by that soldier stationed at Fort Independence... a soldier named none other than Edgar Allan Poe.

Commercial Wharf

The Flying Dutchman of Boston...
the Curious Ghost Ship
of Commercial and Long Wharf

The History

Commercial Wharf in Boston is a popular mecca for leisure boats that dock in the Boston Harbor. The wharf is one of many that dot the shoreline of Boston and provide a glimpse of Boston's maritime past.

Commercial Wharf, sometimes called Granite Wharf at its outset, was constructed in the 1830s during the height of the Atlantic shipping boom. The wharf served as home for the many clipper ships that entered the harbor, trading and selling international wares to the merchants and citizens of Boston.

The wharf protruded 1,100 feet from the North End of Boston and was one hundred sixty feet wide. It was populated by numerous businesses of the day and was home to more than thirty granite storehouses. Built at a cost of $500,000, the wharf sparkled as a gem among wharves in America. The spectacle of the wharf was like none ever seen, teeming with trade from South America, Africa, and India. Many businesses left the nearby wharves to take up residence in the new wharf—and it was so immense that fleets of ships actually passed under it on their treks out to sea.

Commercial Wharf inspired other builders to renovate existing wharves and construct new wharves that rivaled it. Over time, as the clipper ship trade diminished, the wharf lost some of its luster, but still remained an important component of the North End.

Currently, the wharf is lined with moorings for speedboats and yachts. It's also home to condominiums that enjoy a beautiful view of the water vistas that surround Boston. These condos even incorporate some of the original warehouses that were built in the mid nineteenth century. Restaurants and businesses also take up residence at the Wharf, bringing with it a lot of tourist traffic.

Slightly south of Commercial Wharf is the equally historic Long Wharf. Construction on this wharf was lead by Oliver Noyes and was completed in 1710. It served as a port for ships during the early days of Boston's commercial port boom. The wharf extended the once commercially important King Street, allowing it to reach toward the ocean.

As times changed and Boston became part of the United States, King Street became State Street and the importance of the wharf deepened. During the middle of the fur trade and the height of the China trade, Long Wharf became one of the most prominent shipping posts in the world. By the mid 1800s, Long Wharf rivaled Commercial Wharf as an important mooring in Boston. The wharf extended about a third of a mile into the ocean and was about two hundred feet wide. More than seventy storehouses were stationed along the wharf.

Currently, Long Wharf is stationed at the end of Boston's financial district. Much like Commercial Wharf, it draws various tourists and visitors, who moor their ships or walk near the waterways, enjoying one of Boston's most beautiful views.

The Mystery

Commercial and Long wharves remains an attractive mainstay on the Boston coastline. Any visit to the memorable wharf conjures up memories of the glorious ship industry of yore.

However, occasionally a glimpse of that past manifests itself off these shores. According to authors Joseph Mont and Marcia Weaver in *Ghosts of Boston*, Boston's old shipping past caught up to itself in 1974.

It began on a slightly foggy night, at Long Wharf, as the crew of a local fishing boat climbed aboard their small craft hoping to go on a late night excursion. After boarding the ship and checking their gear, they made their way off of the wharf, hoping to engage in an enjoyable evening sail.

All seemed right that night and little appeared out of the ordinary. Suddenly, without warning, sirens and horns rang on the ship. A ship, approaching from the waters beyond Commercial Wharf, appeared on the radar emerging suddenly from the depths of the fog.

The small fishing craft scrambled to evade the fast approaching ship. It dodged it in the nick of time. Passing right past the ship was a decrepit British frigate that looked as if it had not seen the light of day in two hundred years.

Stunned, the crew of the vessel had no idea what to do. They continued their voyage, baffled by what had transpired. Perhaps unsure of what to make of the ship and maybe thinking it to be a mirage, the crew continued on and once again brushed past the ancient ship without warning.

Peering at the ship, the crew noticed that the decaying vessel appeared deserted, sailing under its own power as if in search of a crew. And, just as quickly as it came, it disappeared into the night-time sky, never to be seen again.

Exactly what the crew saw that evening remains to be seen. According to Mont and Weaver, the crew reported the strange occurrence to the Coast Guard, which responded to the call, but did not engage in deeper investigation. The ghost ship has never appeared again quite in that form, though many ship owners report seeing unusual ships along the Boston coast that seem to disappear.

Although the story has never been fully investigated, it is interesting to note that at least two similar, well-known British frigates have been associated with Boston and have disappeared in Massachusetts

Bay. The first, and perhaps best known of these ships, was the HMS Somerset—the ship was made famous in Longfellow's poem "The Midnight Ride of Paul Revere." The ship patrolled Boston Harbor on the eve of the Revolutionary War. It was the ship that Paul Revere passed in his effort to leave Boston and warn the countryside that the British soldiers were marching to Concord and Lexington. This ship proved a formidable foe in the harbor, complete with many cannons that were aimed at the city. During the Revolutionary War, the ship saw action and eventually ran aground off of Provincetown in 1776. The once proud ship was lost at sea. Maybe the ghost ship was the former British frigate attempting to return to port.

Or perhaps it was the French frigate, the Magnifique, that resembled the British ships of the day. This wooden ship was once a wonderful French Man-of-War, complete with seventy-two guns. It was moored in Boston as part of a French fleet of ships that still remained in America following the Revolutionary War. The ship was in poor condition following the war and many historians believe John Paul Jones was going to take the cannons and use them on a ship being constructed as a gift for France. Manned by an American pilot at the time, the Magnifique struck a sandbar near Lovell's Island in Boston Harbor in August 1782. Although all the crew survived, the ship descended to the murky depths, and, according to rumors, took a fortune of gold to the bottom (although no evidence has been found to support that). Is it possible that this ship still patrols the water off the city, looking for the crew that was forced to abandon ship?

Did the crew members in 1974 see a ghostly spirit of one of these ships? Perhaps. Or was it just a mixture of well-placed fog with an overly dark night? It may be hard to tell. But, one thing is for sure – Boston has been an important harbor for more than 350 years. In that time, numerous ships found their final resting place on the shoals and amid the depths of Boston Harbor. Perhaps there is one that still wanders the coastline of Beantown, hoping to find its final mooring amid the speedboats and yachts somewhere between Commercial and Long Wharf.

Gallop's Island

The Tiny Haunted Island...

The History

One of the lesser-known islands in the Boston Harbor island chain is a twenty-three acre isle named Gallop's Island. The island, located in the center of the harbor between George's and Long islands, overlooks the main channel of Boston Harbor and has a unique history all its own. Through many centuries, it has housed a restaurant, several military posts, and a quarantine station.

The island was first explored by the Native Americans, who visited the island shores up until the 1600s. The island later became home to a man named John Gallop, a harbor pilot who helped navigate ships through the harbor.

During the eighteenth and early nineteenth century, the island was farmed extensively. Business took over the island in the 1830s, as entrepreneurs built an inn and restaurant on the tiny isle. Drawing upon stories of pirates and buried treasure, these business owners made the island a local tourist trap of the day.

The outbreak of the Civil War in 1861 ended these lazy days and the island became used by the Union Army. Nearly 3,000 Union soldiers lived on the island, including members of the Massachusetts 54th regiment, the African-American unit that fought valiantly during the Civil War and is celebrated in the movie Glory.

Once the war ended, the island remained in relative obscurity. However, in the early 1900s, Gallop's Island again became an important spot in the city of Boston. When a smallpox epidemic ravaged the city in 1901, a hospital was established on the island for infected patients. Many men suffering from smallpox in Boston were shuttled to the island where they were quarantined, despite the protests of Bostonians who thought that such a hospital might become more like the prisons found on similar islands. During the course of the two-year epidemic, about one hundred forty-two patients were sent to the Gallop's Island hospital. The hospital helped prevent the spread of smallpox throughout the city and the patients there experienced an eleven percent mortality rate.

When the United States entered World War I, the island became used as a prison. Soldiers from German merchant ships captured during battle were detained on the island until the end of the war. Around the same time, an immigration station was established on the island as well.

In the 1920s and 1930s, Dr. Sweeny, one of the doctors stationed on the island, established a beautifying project there. With the help of the Civilian Conservation Corps, more than 2,500 fruit trees, flowering trees, shrubs, and hedges were planted throughout the island, which can still be seen today.

During World War II, soldiers were stationed on Gallop's Island as well, learning to operate radio equipment and cook for the army. The army also established a main street that ran the length of the island to allow soldiers to travel.

Although the island is no longer open to the public, the history of the island is still evident. The remains of the beautifying project and various buildings can still be seen on the island. And there may even be "other" reminders of a past gone by.

The Mystery

A variety of mysteries surround the island, some earthy and some seemingly not. According to legends made popular during the 1800s, a pirate named Long Ben Avery supposedly explored the shore. During one trip, Avery is believed to have carried a fortune in diamonds to the island and buried it in a spot long since forgotten. Plenty of attempts to find the treasure have been made, most during the 1800s. Nothing was ever found.

The island is also associated with pirate lore of another sort. Captain Kidd is thought to have visited the island as well during one of his excursions to the New England shore. Some people believe that his legendary treasure was buried on this island at some point in time. Like Avery's treasure, no proof has ever surfaced to support this idea.

Visitors to the island, however, do report the isle is a source of some strange energy. Those who sense the paranormal report experiencing strong feelings while traversing the island. Some claim the energy connects from those who have departed the earth when the island was used as a quarantine station, while others are not too sure where the energy comes from. Yet, many island-goers have felt this presence when they've set foot on the island.

While Gallop's Island is now closed to the public, perhaps some visitors still come back. It is possible that they wish to enjoy the shallow shores one last time. Or perhaps the visitor is a famous pirate from centuries ago, hoping to unearth some buried treasure.

This view from Boston Harbor shows Boston Harbor's islands in the distance. Several of the islands, including ones used during the expansion of Logan Airport, may be haunted by ghosts.

George's Island

Boston's Famous Ghost...
the Lady in Black

The History

George's Island is a peaceful isle located in Boston Harbor. It is a favorite stop among residents and tourists alike and is a common field trip destination for schools in late spring. As part of the Harbor Islands State Park, George's Island may be reached by a ferry that seasonally travels from Long Wharf in Boston to the island.

The twenty-eight acre island is a refuge of sorts. Though small, the island is home to jetties, some beach combing areas, and precocious sea gulls. The island has a long history in Boston. It was first used by early settlers as farmland. However, as times changed and wars occurred, the island became more strategic, and in 1825, the United States government took over the island and established Fort Warren as a coastal base.

The granite fort was built on the island in 1833. Owned by the government from its inception until 1958, the fortress served to protect the city of Boston and surrounding islands for nearly a century. It served a variety of functions in that time: from training camp, to sentry post, to a prison for Confederate soldiers. During the harsh days of the Civil War, when most prison conditions were considered inhospitable at best, the penitentiary at Fort Warren proved kinder and healthier than most.

For nearly one hundred fifty years, Fort Warren served the United States military admirably. As a training post and camp for several wars, numerous soldiers came out of the fort in good stead. Although the fort has long stood dormant as a military post, it remains to this day as a formidable landmark of the isle. And, while the military may no longer inhabit the fort, at least one ghost just might.

The Mystery

According to local lore, the fort is haunted by the most famous ghost in Boston — the broken-hearted spirit of a Civil War era woman. Affectionately called the Ghost of the Lady in Black, this spirit has been seen, and more often felt, by numerous travelers to the island.

The legend of this ghostly lady begins in North Carolina, during the height of the Civil War, when Union General Burnside led an attack on Roanoke Island and captured many Confederate soldiers. The prisoners were shipped to Boston and placed in the jail on Fort Warren. Before leaving, one of the prisoners, supposedly a Confederate lieutenant who had been married but a few weeks, successfully sent a message to his beloved bride. He explained that he had been captured and was being sent to Fort Warren on George's Island.

The bride was struck by what happened to her husband and vowed to help him escape from the island. She sent word of her plan to her husband who promised to wait for her rescue. They developed a pre-arranged signal for her arrival and he waited for the plot to unfold.

The lady obtained passage to the city of Hull, just outside of Boston. Once there, she was able to find a southern sympathizer who lent her some men's clothing and a pistol. Disguised as a man, she procured a ship and rowed to the island on a rainy, dark night. Quietly, she was able to evade sentries and arrived at a ditch near the dungeon. She signaled to her husband and managed to get to the top part of the fort.

Once reunited, they devised a plan to dig a tunnel and flee from the fort. The plan went well and some digging occurred. However, perhaps by pure folly, bad planning, or a lack of knowledge related to the fort, the prisoners dug a tunnel that was perilously close to soldiers standing on guard. The sound of the digging eventually caught the attention of sentries who mentioned the strange sound to a superior officer named Colonel Dimmick.

The colonel and some men assumed that an escape plot was underway. They rushed inside the fort and tracked down the prisoners. Once cornered, the lady uncovered her pistol and aimed it directly at the Colonel. She fired the pistol, but the age of the instrument caused the trigger to fail, exploding the powder and killing her new spouse instead.

Grief-stricken and distraught, she was quickly captured by the soldiers and tried as a spy. Once convicted, she was sentenced to hang. However, before she went to the hangman's noose, she did offer one final request to the soldiers and commanders at the fort. She wanted to be hanged as a woman in woman's clothes.

Perhaps, knowing that the fort was filled with men, she figured such clothes were unavailable and hoped to buy some time before she met her fate. Or perhaps she wished to be properly dressed for a heavenly reunion with her husband. The soldiers were able to find some clothing that resembled woman's clothes – though no one knows where the clothes came from (different sources say the clothing was a black dress that came from the warden's wife, a dress stitched from curtains from the mess hall, or some old robes in the fort). Whatever the source, the clothes were placed on her and she was hanged as a woman.

While the newlywed may have lost her life, it was hardly the last time she was spotted on the fort. Evidence of her ghost has been spotted many times on the island.

Shortly after her death, soldiers reported seeing female footprints made in snow that start in no particular place and end in no particular place. According to island historian Edward Rowe Snow, several years before the onset of World War II, a soldier was practicing maneuvers on the fort. Reportedly, as the soldier scaled one of the ladders near the capture sight, he was told by a mysterious voice not to enter a nearby room.

Not knowing where it came from and probably aware of the local rumors, he didn't dare defy the ghostly spirit.

Other evidence of the famous lady has also been reported. Snow mentions that many recorded court martial proceedings describe the ghost. Soldiers have left their post because of the ghost and have even made attempts to shoot at the ghost with no avail.

Almost anyone who visits the island may encounter the tale of the Lady in Black. It is still often told by park rangers lecturing visitors to the island. While the famous lady occasionally still appears and recent efforts have been made to videotape her – though no reported encounters have occurred over the last few years – she remains the most-well known ghost in Boston. People flock to George's Island in hopes of a chance encounter or a slight glimpse of the woman who roams the isle, still in search of her husband and a way to escape the island, permanently.

Governor's Island

Boston's First Ghost...

The History

Governor's island is perhaps the most historically well-visited island of the harbor chain. The first Europeans to visit the island were the Puritans, who arrived from England during the 1630s.

John Winthrop, the Puritan leader, settled the island shortly after the Puritans' arrival in Boston. He agreed to lease the isle from the settlement at Boston in exchange for goods raised on the island. Winthrop established a small farm and soon the first fruit trees in America were planted there. When John Winthrop died, officials in Boston agreed to carry on his commitment with later relatives of the Winthrop family, and the property passed through several generations of Winthrops.

The island occasionally saw other occupants, but remained primarily in the Winthrop name into the 1700s. In 1744, the city of Boston decided to place a battery of cannons on the island to protect the city against French ships that were lurking off the coast. The cannons saw a little action in the French and Indian War that followed in the early 1760s. During the Revolutionary War, the cannons remained on the island. It saw minimal action, but it was the landing spot of five British ships swept ashore during a windstorm. It is likely that these ships were preparing to attack Patriot positions during the siege of Boston from 1775 to 1776. The lack of British armaments and the support of these ships eventually forced the British to evacuate the city.

In 1798, construction began on a fort for Governor's Island. The fort, dubbed Fort Warren, helped protect Boston against British warships during the War of 1812. In the 1830s, the fort was renamed Fort Winthrop – with the name Fort Warren being adopted elsewhere in the Boston Harbor island chain – and held a small garrison of men throughout the 1800s. The military discussed housing more men at the island, but never did. Eventually, by the early 1900s, the army had virtually abandoned the island, though the fort still existed. In 1902, an explosion occurred at the fort, killing several island-goers. As a result, the government closed the fort and removed munitions. A few people adopted the island as their unofficial home soon after, acting as island squatters, but were forced to move when the local park department decided to beautify the island. During a typhoid fever scare of 1913, the water source at the island was deemed dangerous, and capped, though it now appears the water may have posed no threat.

The island remained quiet in the 1930s when it perhaps met its most grand moment in history. It became part of the plan to expand the airport in Boston. And, soon enough, Governor's Island became connected to the mainland and succumbed to the expansion of Logan Airport in 1946. There it remains to this day, a subtle reminder of a city gone by, that is greeted by thousands of visitors each day.

The Mystery

Although Governor's Island may not exist as it once had, it still remains the source of an odd ghost story. According to legendary New England author Edward Rowe Snow, the island gave rise to the first reported ghost sighting in Massachusetts.

John Winthrop, island owner, reported the story second-hand. He learned of the strange encounter straight from the source — three men who were sailing near the island on January 18, 1644. As the men stood on the deck of their ship, looking toward the vicinity of Governor's Island and the settlement of Boston, the ocean began to churn. A set of strange lights emerged from the depths of the chilled winter water. Before their eyes, the men watched as the lights transformed into the shape of a man.

Based on Snow's account in *The Islands of Boston Harbor*, the ghostly man spoke to the three sailors. He wanted one of the sailors to join him. The sailors became awestruck. Moments later, the strange apparition descended into the depths never to be seen again.

The waters around Boston have been home to many strange stories and creatures. What might have been this one been? An early explorer lost? Or possibly a sailor whose life was taken by the sea? Maybe, one day, the ghost will show itself again and we might truly find out the source of Boston's first recorded ghost. Until now, the waters around old Governor's Island remain quiet... except for the low rumble of jets passing overhead.

Lewis Wharf

The Haunted Wharf of the North End...

The History

Lewis Wharf is situated on a beautiful section in the North End of Boston. The wharf has played a long-standing role in history. It was one of the major wharves that served the northern side of Boston for more than one hundred fifty years. The wharf was built in 1836 under the direction of Richard Bond. Glorious ships of the day left the wharf bringing in various goods from international ports

Along the dock stands a large building that is impossible to miss. Called the Pilot House, the building was constructed in 1839. For decades the Pilot House served as a boarding house for ship captains and pilots who stopped in the important port city of Boston. It provided them the chance to catch a good meal, a pint of grog, and an opportunity to catch forty winks before heading back to sea. The Pilot House has served many purposes throughout the years, and has contained stores, restaurants, and private businesses.

Today, the wharf has a different look. It is home to condominiums at the Pilot House and places for people to visit along the wharf, as well as some tourist spots to purchase food and other wares. The Pilot House, and the wharf, are part of the Harbor Walk that takes visitors on a quaint excursion along the edge of Boston Harbor, one of the most important waterways of our country. No trip on the Harbor Walk is complete without a stop at the wharf. It is the source of some of the prettiest views of the ocean in the city… and some of the most interesting stories.

The Mystery

The Pilot House may have been a popular spot with captains and ship pilots in the past, but it appears that some may have never left—ghosts have been spotted in the old building, which appears to be a hotbed of paranormal activity.

The upper floors of the building are thought to still house members of ship crews from years gone by. People who have spent time in the building report hearing unintelligible voices of men permeating the halls. The men appear to be talking, perhaps of voyages gone by. The clink and clatter of glass, with an occasional smash, also have been known to punctuate the night, heralding a rowdy day of old. Occasionally, a loud voice or smattering of laughter is also heard among the muted voices.

On the first floor, where restaurants have been located, the ghost of a lady appears from time to time. Dressed in white, she walks through the kitchen visiting the restaurant. Although she is seen intermittently, she typically makes her presence known by moving kitchen items and closing doors. Perhaps she was a cook from the past, visiting the kitchen while trying to prepare a feast for modern visitors.

The phantom lady is one of several ghosts to make themselves known in the former Pilot House. Throughout the building, shadowy figures and eerie voices seem to pass through the halls, sometimes opening doors to enter or leave the building. These figures may be patrons from the past, searching for a room to stay in or a bar to lounge in. Sometimes, there are no figures at all, just the patter of footsteps creaking up stairs.

Even outside the wharf, visitors and residents alike have claimed to see or feel something unnatural along the wharf. Often, during strolls on moonless nights, or nights when a thick fog has rolled into the city, wharf-goers profess to feeling as if they are not alone. Sometimes, this presence actually manifests itself in the form of an old sailor or captain wandering the wharf in search of a room at the Pilot House or maybe even a ship to board. Other times, the presence surfaces over the water, floating on the crest of waves appearing as orbs over the ocean.

Who exactly these people are remains known only to the past. But, it appears that some captains may never have shaken their love for the city. It is quite possible that they visit from time to time when their ship once again rolls in.

Long Island

The Scarlet Ghost...
the Haunting of Long Island

The History

Long Island is one of the many islands that comprise the Boston Harbor chain. Located in the Quincy Bay section, the island is connected to the mainland by a causeway that is more than 4,000 feet long.

Native Americans were the first people to inhabit the island, using it for farming and fishing until the 1630s. In 1634, Puritan leaders from the town of Boston purchased the land, along with Hogg and Deer islands, for much needed resources. At the time, Long Island teemed with animals and wood, and it contained soil perfect for farming. Colonial Bostonians used the island primarily for a source of wood during the 1600s, but it also acted as a temporary animal shelter during the corn-growing season. Pigs, goats, and other farm animals that might feast on the corn were penned on the island while the stalks grew.

The latter half of the seventeenth century brought much activity to the island. Colonial farmers began renting land, and in 1676, colonists rounded up Christianized Native Americans from Natick and Marlboro during the midst of the King Phillip's War. A small contingent of these Native Americans, all of whom sympathized with the English, became forced to live on the island. Many members of the tribes perished there from the lack of resources and shelter. The island transformed from a supposed safe haven to a prison for Native Americans a year later, as colonists feared the Native Americans were interacting with French settlers in a quest to cause a war in New England.

In 1690, much of the island was purchased by a man named John Nelson. A privateer by nature – and a man who once led a revolt against Massachusetts Royal Governor Edmund Andros, who had revoked the colony's charter – he became the first of many owners to develop the land. By the mid 1700s, the island contained a variety of houses, pastures, waterways, and common. With each passing owner, the island changed names as well, at one time becoming Nelson's Island and Apthorp Island.

In the 1760s, the island came under the jurisdiction of British occupying forces who had entered Boston to ensure the security and peace of British interests, particularly in the wake of protests over British laws. These protests would eventually lead to the Revolutionary War. By 1768, the British forces had designated the island for animal use. Cattle, sheep, and pigs grazed on the island, and hay was harvested to feed horses in Boston proper.

The island became a hot spot during the revolution. In July 1775, American soldiers raided the island, claiming all of the British animals and capturing seventeen British soldiers. They soon erected two cannons on the island, which became known as the "Long Island Battery" during the Revolution. The cannon fired on British ships during the end of the British occupation of Boston, leading to the eventual withdrawal of British ships from the harbor islands.

Following the war, the island was again sold to a private owner and became known officially as Long Island once again. A lighthouse was built on the island in 1794 and reconstructed in 1819. The island served as fortification for Boston during the War of 1812, becoming the home of Fort Strong. In the 1840s, a group of Portuguese fisherman moved to the island, creating a small village. Within a few years, the island also became home to a small hotel and was transformed into a recreational area until 1860 when the country was on the brink of a Civil War. Camp Wrightman, a military fort, was built on the island. Members of the 3rd and 4th Massachusetts Regiments trained on the island and took part in many important battles during the War between the States. In the 1870s, gun batteries were placed on the island and in the 1880s, an almshouse for men opened there as well. The city of Boston took control of the island in 1885 and has held it since that time. The island was later the location of a home for unwed mothers, a hospital for chronic illnesses, and a radar station during the Cold War era. The island still contains an automated light that is maintained by the Coast Guard.

Today, the island is part of the Boston Harbor island chain, complete with several buildings and military complexes. Unlike many of the city's harbor islands, Long Island is now closed to the public.

The Mystery

Long Island's history has proven diverse and interesting. It has served multiple purposes to the Boston community. With such a lengthy service time, there is little doubt that an air of mystery might linger on the island.

The main mystery dates back to the Revolutionary War era. Originally recounted by famed Boston historian Edward Rowe Snow, the source of the mystery dates back to 1776. As the British navy and army began a slow retreat from Boston, preparing to leave the city and begin an occupation of New York, several ships came under Patriot cannon fire from the island and surrounding parts of Boston. Night skirmishes and day fighting proved devastating for the British army that had already suffered an unlikely defeat in the city of Boston.

William Burton, thought to be a British loyalist in the city, had joined the British army probably during the waning days of Boston's occupation. As the soldiers were evacuated from the city, his wife, Mary, joined him on one of the British ships. While the ship prepared to move to safer waters, a cannonball believed to be from the Long Island Battery ripped across the bow. The shot was devastating, smashing into Mary's head. The blow proved fatal and Mary sat on the deck, taking her last breaths. As she bid the world farewell, she asked her husband to promise not to bury her at sea, but to grant her a proper burial on land.

Her husband agreed. During the midst of the cannonade, Burton's ship raised a flag of truce. The American soldiers on shore relented and waited as a small rowboat made its way to shore. When the boat arrived, William disembarked, carrying the body of his wife, draped in a red cloth.

Burton asked permission to bury the body on shore. The American soldiers agreed and allowed Burton to bury her on a section of the island called East Head. A wooden cross was placed on her grave and one of the American soldiers placed her name on it to serve as a marker when Burton returned to Boston.

However, Burton never returned to Boston. The grave of Mary Burton disappeared as weather and age slowly decayed the wooden marker. Island-goers, who had heard the story, tried to commemorate the grave by placing a pile of stones where they thought she was buried. While it appeared to some Bostonians that Mary's memory might slowly fade with the passage of time, her memory proved to be quite alive.

In 1804, a group of fishermen found themselves washed up on the island. Seeking shelter in a nearby building, they quickly built a fire. Moments later, they were surprised to hear the sound of a person screaming coming from a hill nearby. They rushed out of the building in time to see the figure of a woman, draped in a red cloth. She ambled past them, blood dripping from her head, and disappeared into the stale ocean air. About eight years later, soldiers stationed at then Fort Strong reported other ghostly sightings while on patrol. Rumors started to spread about the ghostly vision of a woman dressed in scarlet visiting the fort. Following the war, the rumors subsided … until the 1890s, when a man named William Liddell, a private on the island, spotted the same lady. She came toward him with a distinct moan forming on her lips. Eventually, she disappeared into the chilly Atlantic air.

Who is this woman? Most witnesses believe it is Mary Burton, visiting the island while waiting for her husband to return from England. How long will she wait? It all depends on if the ghost of William Burton returns.

Nix's Mate

The Island Swallowed
by the Ocean...

The History

Amid the many islands in Boston Harbor rests a small island called Nix's Mate (sometimes known as Nixes Mate). More of pebble than an actual island, Nix's Mate is marked by a large pyramid beacon used by sailors as a navigational aid when they enter Boston Harbor. The island, now a shell of its former self, has played an interesting role in Boston history.

The island is about six miles off the shore of Boston and was once comprised of twelve acres of land. In 1636, John Gallop purchased the island from the city of Boston. Living on what is now known as Gallop's Island, Gallop used the fertile acreage of Nix's Island to graze sheep. For the next century, the island also served as a quarry, supplying ballast for ships and slate for the surrounding region. However, the island always took a pounding from the ocean and slowly dissolved into the sea.

In the 1800s, it became evident that the island's erosion posed a problem for Boston Harbor. Because Nix's Mate was located at the meeting point of three major channels, the decay of the landscape caused the potential for sandbars to form. Residents constructed a wall on the island to counteract this problem, and by 1805, Bostonians added the beacon to Nix's Mate in an effort to help sailors pilot their way in and out of the harbor.

In 1832, the U.S. government took control of the beacon, creating a sturdier pyramid from the old wall. It was struck by lightning and burned down in 1841, but was rebuilt shortly after. The beacon has been rebuilt several times. During the years, slate shingles and concrete were added to help strengthen the beacon from the power of the Atlantic Ocean.

In that time, the once twelve-acre island has been reduced to a mere one-acre. During certain times of year, the tide can almost completely cover the once proud sheep pasture, leaving a two hundred-foot piece of Nix's Mate stretching ten feet into the air visible only to passing ships.

The Mystery

Nix's Mate may be the tiniest of the Boston Harbor islands, but its history rivals that of the largest islands. The evolution of the island as a landmark in the harbor points to the diverse history of the region. The island itself has served not only as a beacon, but a burial ground and a prison of sorts.

The origin of the name Nix's Mate has been obscured by time. Some scholars point to the Dutch phrase "nixie shmalt," which refers to the call of water spirits. New England traditionalists prefer a far more poetic and eerie story. They point to a legend that says the island is named for the first mate of a ship captain named Nix. Nix had disappeared at sea and some claimed he had been murdered. Nix's first mate stood accused of the murder. Although he declared his innocence, Bostonians found him guilty and hanged the mate on the island.

Right before he was hanged, the mate declared his innocence once again. As a final testament against the false accusations, Nix's mate vowed that time would prove his innocence. He promised that if he were truly innocent, the ocean itself would devour the island.

No one is certain if this story is true. The facts surrounding the event have been lost to history. However, there is no doubt that the sea has indeed swallowed the island slowly during the past three centuries.

If the possible origin for the name was not enough to intrigue paranormal enthusiasts, Nix's Mate has even more tragedy surrounding it — tragedy that has existed on the island for several hundred years.

The main source of this tragedy involves the pirates who appeared in the Atlantic waterways during the seventeenth and eighteenth century. Feasting on ships traveling throughout the English colonies, pirates posed a particular problem to coastal port cities such as Boston. In order to thwart the deeds of such buccaneers, city officials were particularly harsh on suspected pirates. Leniency was denied most pirates who ventured into the city. The consequences of being caught and convicted of piracy could be particularly gruesome.

One of the main methods of chasing pirates from the waterways was to hang them on one of the islands and leave their body on display for months or years to serve as a warning to other pirates. Nix's Mate, as well as Bird Island in the harbor, were the main two islands to serve this purpose.

At least three pirates suffered such a fate on Nix's Mate. The most famous of these pirates was a sea dog named William Fly. Fly began his career as a boatswain in spring 1726, when he sparked a revolt on the slave ship Elizabeth traveling from Jamaica to West Africa. Once he gained control of the ship, he renamed it Fame's Revenge and began a short-lived pirate career, turning the ship toward the American coast. Fly and his pirate crew preyed on ships off the coast of North Carolina and New England, capturing about five ships before being caught off the coast of Newburyport, Massachusetts. Fly was later brought to Boston to be tried for the crime. Known for his harsh ways – he supposedly punished people by whipping them beyond recognition – he found no friends in Boston. Fly was quickly convicted and sentenced to hang on Nix's Mate.

Following Fly's conviction, Puritan leader Cotton Mather asked the buccaneer to seek public repentance. Fly ignored the request and instead met the hangman's noose with the disdain that was typical of those times. According to legend, he noticed that the hangman was a tenderfoot who knew little about noose tying. Growing quickly impatient with the man's lack of skill, Fly snapped the rope from the man's hands and tied the knot for himself before being hanged.

Following the execution, Fly's body was put in chains and left to hang for the rest of the pirate world to see.

Fly's parting words were believed to be a reprimand to other sailors to treat their crew well. Eventually buried on the island with two other pirates, it is believed that Fly's spirit has lingered on to help ensure his words were carried out. On the island that is slowly succumbing to the ocean, sailors have reported seeing mysterious lights, hearing blood curdling screams and uneasy laughs, as well as awkward whispers. Many speculate that the spirit of the violent pirate roams the island patrolling the land and calling to all sailors as they pass by. Is he reminding the sailors of his famous final words? Or is he still serving as a reminder of the perils of piracy along the Atlantic shores?

Part Three:

Amid the Graveyards

Boston's graveyards are the final resting place for many of America's best and brightest historical figures. Men and women, from Paul Revere, to Cotton Mather, to John Hancock, and even a woman thought to be Mother Goose are just a handful of renown people who claim Boston as their final resting place. A quick walk through any of these cemeteries will yield a virtual American Hall-of-Fame.

Many of the cemeteries in the city are actually old burying grounds. These were places where individual plots are rarely the norm. Multiple people were buried within the same plot in most of the burying grounds. Often, the plots with headstones remind us of the last person to be buried there.

While the cemeteries may be filled with famous names, the grave-yards themselves are landmarks for other reasons as well. Strange histories, glorious monuments, and interesting politics all mark the cemeteries found throughout the city. Many have stories that have stood the test of time.

And, what would a cemetery be without a ghost story or two. Luckily, in Boston, you will find at least one popular legend – and sometimes many more – associated with the burying grounds found here…

The Central Burying Ground, located in Boston Common
is believed to have at least one active ghost.

Central Burying Ground

The Burying Ground in the Center of Town...

The History

While Boston Common has played host to many sites of both natural and supernatural phenomena, it is also home to one of the most interesting cemeteries in Boston. Located in a corner of the Common, the Central Burying Ground contains many old gravesites.

Land for the cemetery was purchased by the town in 1756. The earliest burials included British soldiers who were stationed in the city during the occupation of Boston and the Revolutionary War. In fact, many of the British soldiers who fell during the Battle of Bunker Hill were buried in a portion of the cemetery.

Between the early 1790s and 1815, numerous tombs were constructed on the site. In that same century, part of the graveyard was appropriated by the city and used to build a walkway. The graves of many former residents still exist under the walkway. The cemetery was further reconstructed in the late 1800s, when the city built the first subway in America. As a result, between nine hundred and 1,100 graves were moved and relocated into mass tombs. These tombs are still visible in the burying ground.

The Central Burying Ground is the final resting place of many famous people, including America's first renown composer, William Billings, who wrote numerous hymns. The cemetery is also the home to a member of the Continental Congress named Stephen Higginson and Gilbert Stuart, who painted the famous portrait of George Washington that graces the dollar bill. Finally, a renown chef named Jean Baptiste Julien is interred in this site. He created the meal known today as Julien soup.

The Mystery

While Boston Common itself is a graveyard of sorts to countless people, this actual cemetery is the final resting place of more than 1,600 residents of Boston—as well as a host of other worldly travelers.

For most people who visit the cemetery, the ghosts make themselves known in mysterious ways. Passersby who claim to have experienced these ghostly visitors describe a sense of uneasiness or discomfort, as if someone or something is watching them. They may not witness a ghost, but claim that "something" is nearby.

For others, the feeling is much more tangible. Visitors to the graveyard have reported seeing shadowy figures appear nearby, often near trees. Some people have associated the figures with the former hanging victims who met their end on the Boston Common gallows. The figures disappear or dissolve when people look right at them. Occasionally, the shadows become slightly more mischievous. They have been accused of poking people in the back, rattling keys, and even brushing up against shoulders. Some people roaming the graveyard have reported being grabbed from behind by an unseen force.

There is one well known tale about a ghostly encounter in the cemetery. Joe O'Shea in an article called "A Spirited Tour of Boston," relates a story from Jim McCabe, a legendary ghost and graveyard expert in Boston. According to McCabe, in the 1970s, a retired dentist was passing near the Central Burying Ground. Without any cause or warning, he was suddenly poked in the back. He ignored the source of the poke, perhaps figuring it was his imagination, until he felt a large tug on his collar. He turned around and came face to face with a little girl with long red hair, a dirty dress, and a shallow complexion.

The dentist shrugged off the girl's rudeness and turned around, only to come face to face with the girl immediately as he turned. She was surely no ordinary girl. Alarmed – and no doubt a little distressed by the turn of events, the dentist raced from the burying ground as fast as he could. Ironically, before he could go, he felt the girl reach into his pockets and remove his car keys. He saw the girl shake the keys in the air and then drop them. A moment later, she disappeared into the cool air of Boston.

Although this girl has never been spotted again, there are some in Boston who wander in the burying ground and wonder if she, or someone else, might return to the city again. For those who are daring enough to find out, it is a good idea to hold onto your car keys.

Copp's Hill Burying Ground is in the heart of the famous North End.
It has quite a hallowed history in this part of Boston.

Copp's Hill Burying Ground

The Cemetery on the Hill...

The History

In the 1660s, the residents of what is now known as the North End of Boston realized they needed to build a cemetery. They appealed to a man named William Copp, a resident cobbler, who owned a large plot of land along a hilltop. The land, used as a location for windmills since the arrival of the first settlers in the 1630s, had been once dubbed Windmill Hill. To the residents of Boston, it proved an ideal location for a burial ground. Copp sold the land to the citizens of Boston to provide for a graveyard.

The graveyard, originally called the North Burying Ground, is now named for its original owner and is dubbed Copp's Hill Burying Ground. It lies on the pastoral setting overlooking the Charles River. Long known as the highest point in the North End, it has served as the final resting spot of residents from this section of Boston for centuries.

The names do not jump out at most visitors – there are certainly no Reveres, Hancocks, and Adams buried here – however many of the names have a significant local flavor. The most famous residents are located in a tomb near the Charter Street entrance, on the bottom slope of the hill. Here, visitors find the Mather tombs, where the graves of early Puritan preachers Increase and Cotton Mather can be found. This father and son duo grew famous for their strict adherence to Puritanical laws and their fire and brimstone speeches. The Mathers gained a degree of notoriety during the Salem Witch Trials. The Puritan officials presiding over the affair used Cotton's 1689 book, *Memorable Providences, Relating to Witchcraft and Possessions*, as a means to determine the identity of witches in the vicinity of Salem. Once the Mathers realized the folly of the trials and the political nature that drove the forces in the town, they tried to intercede and eventually helped put a stop to the ordeal.

Also located in the burying ground is the grave of Edward Hartt. Although his name may not skip off the tongue, Hartt was a shipbuilder who constructed the U.S.S. Constitution, one of America's first warships. The Constitution gained fame during the Barbary Wars and the War of 1812, as cannon balls, shot at the ultra-thick hull, bounced off with ease, earning the ship the nickname Old Ironsides.

Another memorable figure buried in Copp's Hill is Prince Hall. Commemorated with a large marker along the Snow Street entrance, Hall's memorial stone is hard to miss. Standing like a giant column rising from the grass, the memorial commemorates the legacy of this freed slave from nearby Medford. Hall was granted his freedom when he decided to join the American army during the Revolutionary War. Once the war was over, Hall returned to Boston and became an important leader in the African-American community. He helped establish the first Masonic lodge for African-Americans in 1784, and he also helped open the first African-American school for children in Boston. His tomb is located in a section of the cemetery where hundreds of African-American residents were buried at the time.

Not too far from Hall's memorial lies the gravestone of a man named Daniel Malcolm. His is the tallest in a row of several gravestones in the vicinity. Malcolm, a merchant in the 1700s, became a member of the Sons of Liberty, the Patriot organization that opposed British taxes and their rule in Boston. Merchants such as Malcolm and John Hancock found ways to avoid the taxes. At one point, Malcolm smuggled five dozen casks of wine into the port city without paying the obligatory tax. The British became incensed by such antics and often had their eye out for him. When Malcolm went on his final departure from the region, he was buried deep in the ground to ensure that the British would not be able to reach him. Alas, many years later the British did remember him while camped out on the hill during the Revolution. Malcolm's headstone became a favorite spot for British soldiers to practice their musketry. Malcolm's stone still contains small, unmistakable bullet holes that harken back to the days when the redcoats used it for musket practice.

Behind Malcolm's tomb, diagonally to the left along an iron fence, is the gravestone of another North Ender named Robert Newman. Like Malcolm, Newman also was a member of the Sons of Liberty. He participated in various events to thwart the British rule in the city. However, he is best known in these parts as working as the sexton in the Old North Church. Many historians believe Newman raised the two lanterns in the steeple of the church to signal Patriots that the British were marching by way of the ocean.

Also interred in the burying ground are members of the Worthylake family. This is the same family that perished on Boston Light during its opening years of existence. Several members of the family have their final resting place here.

Another interesting tomb, located near the Hull Street entrance of the cemetery, is simply known as William Clark's tomb. However, visitors to the cemetery should not be fooled. William Clark's body has been long vacated from the tomb — his final grave site is not exactly known. In its place rests the body of a man named Samuel Winslow, who claimed the tomb for himself.

Several other interesting gravestones peak up from the grounds. Copp's own children are buried in the cemetery, located in a plot near the hill's peak. Many of the other stones belong to regular North Enders from the past, who have helped to make this section of Boston an important landmark to the city.

The hill itself – both the cemetery and surrounding landscape – have played various roles in history. Besides the aforementioned location of windmills, the primary role of the hill as a cemetery was superceded during the Revolutionary War. At the time, the British claimed the hill and mounted cannons atop it to defend themselves during the siege of Boston. They trained the cannons squarely onto the surrounding city of Charleston and the thousands of armed Patriots who had gathered their to force the British back to Britain. While the British are remembered for using gravestones as target practice, they also are said to have used the hill to fire upon Americans during the Battle of Bunker Hill (which, ironically, occurred on Breed's Hill).

The British were not the only ones to use the cemetery in multiple ways. In the 1800s, residents decided to use the graveyard as a resource of sorts. More than twenty of the gravestones were removed from the cemetery and used for various projects in the area. At least twenty-two of the stones have been found. Some had been used for the foundation of houses. Others helped take the place of loose roof tiles on area houses. And at least one was used by a local cook as a baking plate

Outside the cemetery, the sloping part of the hill takes you toward Commercial Street. It is interesting to note that two famous events occurred within this vicinity. The famed Brinks Robbery took place here in 1950, when more than $1 million was stolen from the Brinks Company that had offices on the street. A little further down, near the intersection with Commercial Street, is the site of the famous molasses flood of 1919. This tragedy occurred when a tank of molasses exploded, flooding the street. At least twenty-one people and numerous animals died under the flash flood of molasses. The scent of molasses floated in the air for decades after…and some people still claim to smell it on a hot summer day.

The Mystery

Most of Copp's Hill Burying Ground remains a typical burying ground — a landmark to the past and a tourist spot. Some visitors to the hallowed ground feel a strange sensation on the spot, perhaps a testimony to the many souls who have departed the earth, or perhaps related to the tragedy that has surrounded the landscape.

Occasionally, a passerby has claimed to have spotted a phantom shadow or ghost creeping through the cemetery. Often, these supposed spirits are witnessed at dusk. They are typically seen for a moment and then vanish. Other people believe that there are tunnels under the Burying Ground that are haunted by the spirits of those who loved the North End and never left. However, no one has ever found these sub-terranian tunnels.

Exactly who these ghosts might be is unknown and sightings occur so sporadically that it's hard to even predict when they might appear. But for those who have encountered the ghosts, many are sure that they certainly point to the spirits of a North End gone by who are not ready to leave their favorite part of town.

Granary Burying Ground may be the home of a ghost that haunts a nearby landmark. The Franklin cenotaph is located in the center of the picture.

Granary Burying Ground

The Cemetery of the Rich and Famous...

The History

G ranary Burying Ground was opened in 1660 and is considered the third oldest cemetery in Boston. During its history, the graveyard has been known by several names. It was originally named the South Burying Ground because of its location on the southern border of the original Boston settlement. As the colony in Boston expanded, what was once the southern region became more of a midpoint and soon the burying ground was dubbed the Middle Burying Ground. Eventually, it was renamed the Granary Burying Ground for its location near a granary warehouse that once stood in the spot now occupied by Park Street Church.

A short jaunt through the cemetery will reveal a who's who of famous names that appear in the history of Beantown. Entering the cemetery through the Tremont Street entrance, the first noticeable headstone to spot on the right belongs to John Phillips, who served as the first mayor of Boston.

A little beyond his headstone, in the front right section of the cemetery, are the graves of victims related to tensions between the British and colonists that occurred in 1770. One of the graves belongs to a young boy named Christopher Snider, who died from a gunshot fired by a Loyalist protecting his house from colonial antagonists in early 1770. Snider's unfortunate death caused tensions to boil in the city and helped precipitate the infamous "Boston Massacre" that occurred on March 5, 1770. The bodies of the five Patriots killed in this incident – Cripus Attucks, James Caldwell, Patrick Carr, Samuel Gray, and Samuel Maverick – are also buried in this spot.

Just beyond this spot, to the right, rests the tomb of Samuel Adams. A chief agitator between the colonists and the British, Adams almost single-handedly caused the Revolutionary War. As a leader of the Sons of Liberty, Adams typically stirred up trouble between the colonists and the British and he was instrumental in dubbing the incident of March 5th "the Boston Massacre." He persuaded Paul Revere to create an engraving that inaccurately depicts British soldiers firing on a defenseless group of Patriots. It was Adams, and his good friend John Hancock (who is also interred in the cemetery), whom the British hoped to arrest during their march to Concord and Lexington that helped spark the American Revolution.

Perhaps the most interesting headstone in the graveyard rests in the center right section of the cemetery, just beyond the Adams and 1770 gravestones. In memory of Mary Vergoose, who died in 1757, this stone has garnered much attention during the past two centuries. Mary Vergoose was married to a man named Isaac Vergoose. Together, they had ten children, and raised ten more from Isaac's first marriage. Eventually, when Isaac died, Mary moved in with a daughter and reportedly spent her time telling stories to her fourteen grandchildren.

Some local residents claim that Mary's son-in-law was a printer. Although no proof can be found, he reportedly printed a book based on the stories that Mary told her grandchildren and attributed the tales to her, while changing her name slightly. Titled *Songs for the Nursery*, or *Mother Goose's Melodies*, the book contained several of her best tales. However, like many Boston legends, this one may be straight out of fantasy books. No copy of the book has ever been seen and many historians doubt the authenticity of the tale. Still, Boston loves to claim that Mother Goose walked their streets at one time.

Toward the center of the graveyard is a large stone obelisk called the Franklin cenotaph. A group of Bostonians fashioned this memorial in 1827 in honor of Benjamin Franklin's parents, Josiah and Abiah, who are buried in the spot. Benjamin himself lived in Boston as a young lad, but moved to Philadelphia to escape the abusive life he lived with his brother while growing up in the city. Close to the memorial are headstones of other family members related to Benjamin Franklin. At one time the headstone of his uncle, Benjamen, for whom he was named, could be seen in the cemetery. It has since been taken from the site, though no one knows who claimed it.

To the far left center of the cemetery lies a memorial to John Hancock. His memorial is a tall white pillar that lies near the border of the graveyard. During his life, Hancock was the richest man in Boston and gained fame for his ability to stir up Patriots as well as signing the Declaration of Independence with his typical flamboyant style. Hancock's original marker has disappeared over time and has been replaced by the current memorial. Some local residents believe Hancock's final resting place is no longer in the cemetery and that his body may have been removed by grave robbers when minor reconstruction occurred on the cemetery. No truth to that rumor has ever been corroborated. To the right of Hancock's headstone is a small stone with the name of Frank etched across the top. Frank, an African-American, was probably Hancock's slave and worked as a servant to the wealthy man.

In the far left section of the cemetery lies a table tomb originally belonging to "P. Funal." P. Funal immigrated to America from France and became a wealthy merchant in the town. Because his name proved difficult to say and spell, the original stonecutter placed "P. Funal" on the marker. Over time, the words have slowly faded and have been replaced by an updated spelling that is much better known — "Peter Faneuil." He was an important merchant in the city and founded what is now known as Faneuil Hall.

Along the middle of the back section rests the tomb of one of the more famous residents of Revolutionary Boston, that of legend ary Patriot, silversmith, and horseback rider Paul Revere. But, don't let those history books fool you. Revere was not the only horseback rider to warn that the British army was marching to Lexington and Concord. Many other riders rode that night, spreading the alarm. However, when Longfellow wrote his poem, he chose to commemorate only one native son. Ironically, part of Revere's mission was to warn fellow internees Adams and Hancock that the British hoped to arrest them.

The Mystery

A short walk through Granary Burying Ground can leave any passerby with a mixture of emotions. Walking through a cemetery filled with such history is often an overpowering experience and seeing the names of so many famous figures from history causes people to pause as they wander among the gravestones.

However, there is another experience that brings pause as well. No one is exactly sure who or what causes this, but many visitors describe unusual feelings as they pass through the cemetery, as if the past is watching them. Who might these eyes be? Maybe those of a wayward spirit from the past? Or the founders of freedom watching over the contemporary city? No one knows. However, there is a certain degree of comfort thinking that as you pass through the graveyard, you might just be rubbing shoulders with John Hancock, Paul Revere, or perhaps even Mother Goose.

It is also worth noting that the burying ground is located near the Boston Athenaeum. Some local residents believe that a ghost from this burying ground haunts the current building. Who might this ghost be? Well, many believe the ghost is Reverend Thadeus Harris who haunted the original building located blocks from the cemetery (for more on that, check out the chapter about the Boston Athenaeum). However, he is not believed to be buried in this cemetery. So, some people think that a ghost from this cemetery took over the reverend's haunt when the building moved many years ago.

King's Chapel Burying Ground

The Oldest Cemetery in Town...

The History

King's Chapel Burying Ground is the oldest known official cemetery located in Boston. Although no one is quite certain, it is believed that the first known burial occurred on these hallowed grounds shortly after a band of Puritan settlers arrived on the Boston shores in 1630. The cemetery is located next to King's Chapel, an Anglican Church, but the two were not built in conjunction with each other. In fact, land from the cemetery was used for the construction of the chapel. Ironically, many of the earliest people buried in the cemetery are Puritans, who left England because they were at odds with the Anglican church.

Hundreds of people are buried in this burial ground. However, an exact number is unknown. During the one hundred fifty years that Bostonians performed burials at the site, graves sometimes contained as many as twenty people even though only one headstone, if any, was used to mark the grave. For the most part, burials in King's Chapel Burying Ground stopped in 1796 (although it is thought that other remains may have been added, but not noted), except for a few modern priests and clergy who are interred here.

King's Chapel Burying Ground, like many of its day, became a dismal place by the end of the eighteenth century. According to some stories, pieces of caskets and even remains of bodies occasionally pushed through the soil by the early 1800s. As a result, in the first part of the nineteenth century, a gradual process of tending the graveyard began to make it a suitable memorial for the departed. Many of the gravestones were rearranged into rows for purposes of tidying the cemetery. Despite effort to improve the grounds, no one organized the rows in relation to who was buried in the cemetery. Because of this, it is uncertain where the exact remains of people are located within King's Chapel Burying Ground.

The King's Chapel Burying Ground is home to some of Boston's legendary characters. A few people claim that this burying ground might be haunted.

The cemetery is the final resting place of numerous important residents of Boston's past. John Winthrop, the Puritan "founder of Boston," is buried in the cemetery. He is known as one of a number of people who hoped to form a model city among the three hills in

Boston. Winthrop's grave is marked by a bench-like memorial in the far right section of the cemetery.

Mary Chilton, the first female to disembark the Mayflower in 1620, has her final resting place in the cemetery as well. Her tomb is marked across from Winthrop's on the other side of a walkway. Legend has it that Chilton may have been the first person to actually set foot on Plymouth Rock. Although historians doubt the rock was actually a landing point, the annals of American history still like to circulate the tale. It makes for better legends.

William Dawes, a friend of Paul Revere, is also buried within the confines of the cemetery. His tomb is located behind Chilton's, diagonally to the right. Dawes is often forgotten in history, but he assisted Revere in the famous ride on April 18 and 19, 1775, warning the Massachusetts countryside that British soldiers were marching toward Lexington and Concord.

A woman named Elizabeth Pain has a burial plot in the cemetery as well. Her gravestone is located toward the far right, front section of the cemetery. Ornately decorated with a shield containing the letter "A," the gravestone eventually became a legend of its own. Literary scholars believe that her gravestone served as an inspiration to Nathaniel Hawthorne, who was a frequent visitor to the grounds. The gravestone of Hester Pryne, in *The Scarlet Letter*, is described quite similarly, right down to the burial spot — King's Chapel Burying Ground. Although Mrs. Pain's gravestone is likely included in the book, there is no evidence to suggest that Pain herself had any connection to the book, or committed any crime that is similar to the one in *The Scarlet Letter*.

The Mystery

The cemetery has been the source of interesting stories and ghostly speculation for centuries. One of the oddest stories to circulate about the cemetery is that someone was buried alive there. Although it is uncertain how this rumor started, it became quite popular for a time in the past. Bostonians speculated who the person was and were so sure of the identity at that time that the name itself spread like a weed throughout the city (although it has since been lost to history). People came to the cemetery to see for themselves if it was likely someone had been buried alive. Residents believed the story to be true until a doctor came forth saying that he had inspected the body of the supposed person before it was interred in the cemetery. The doctor claimed the body was, indeed, deceased. By verifying that he had seen the body, the doctor officially ended the rumor. Yet another legend – and the deceased name – vanished into the salty landscape of Boston.

Perhaps the most interesting legend involves a supposed grave that is located in the back section of the burying ground. The gravestone is said to bear no name. Buried deep in this spot, according to lore, lies the final resting place of Pirate Captain Kidd.

There is little proof to support this claim. First, it is hard to find any such grave in the back portion of the cemetery. Most of the headstones contain names; and while many names have been worn away by age and weather, none look truly unmarked. Likewise, according to historical records, Captain Kidd was arrested in Boston in 1701 and brought back to England to serve trial. While Kidd proclaimed his innocence to the last, he was eventually hanged. The British authorities then displayed Kidd's body as a warning for other pirates who dared replicate his pirating ways. Most historians agree that Kidd's final remains lay in England, deep in an unmarked grave. Yet, a few people contend that Kidd's body made its way back to Boston.

While it might seem unlikely, according to ghost authors Marcia Weaver and Joseph Mont, there are some grave-goers who swear that Kidd's spirit can be summoned late at night, during the bewitching hour, and seen patrolling Boston's ancient burying ground. This legend has been passed down for many years making some people wonder if Captain Kidd didn't have the heart to leave the city he enjoyed so much.

Part Four:

Pure Fantasy?

Boston has been home to many authors who have spun wild and marvelous tales. Frequent visitors to the city have included Edgar Allan Poe, Nathaniel Hawthorne, Henry Wadsworth Longfellow, Charles Dickens, and Eugene O'Neill, just to name a few. These writers have all helped to make Boston a beacon of the literary world.

However, despite the many famous authors who took up residence here, the city itself has given birth to its share of wild tales. Numerous ghost stories and local legends have emanated from the city. Many have basis in historical fact or can be traced to certain origins. But, occasionally other stories have surfaced that resemble pure fantasy.

The following are two ghostly tales that have been told over the years. While the stories may contain bits of truth, there are many that believe the tales are more the handiwork of imagination than the supernatural.

Check them out…and see what you think.

Peter Rugg used to live on Middle Street, now present day Hanover Street.
Will his ghost one day attempt to return home?

The Legend of Peter Rugg

The Roaming Ghost of Boston...

The History

The year 1770 was a pivotal moment in American history. The thirteen colonies, still under the jurisdiction of the mother country of England, were embroiled in a hotbed of protests against their colonizer. Protests over taxation, imports, and unfair laws abounded through the land.

Boston, more so than any city in the colonies, was at the center of the protests. Led by organized citizens who spoke out against the tyranny of the king, groups like the Sons of Liberty formed and, sparked by Samuel Adams and John Hancock, the groups looked for small events to turn into major issues.

In March 1770, one such event helped send the colonies into a rebellious frenzy. As colonial protestors and British soldiers squared off outside of the Old State House, momentary chaos reigned. Soldiers and citizens sparred, resulting in the infamous incident that was later dubbed the Boston Massacre. Five Americans were eventually left dead because of the situation (and were later buried in the Granary Burying Ground). In a scene memorialized by Paul Revere, colonists throughout the land began to develop rebellion fever. In five more years, the Revolutionary War would begin in earnest, in part spurred by this situation.

The Mystery

Yet, 1770 may have been better known for a more mysterious set of circumstances that occurred on the back roads of Massachusetts. According to legend – though no one is quite sure how this legend developed – the roads leading into Boston became the site of a unique haunting. The details of this particular story are fuzzy and most believers relegate it to mere folklore. However, the story persists to this day, as ghost hunters and folklorists alike pass it down to each new generation.

It is important to note that the story below was recounted by an American writer named William Austin. Putting pen to paper in the early 1800s, he modeled his career after America's first beloved writer, Washington Irving. The style, the characters, even the themes of Austin's tale are similar to those of Irving's. While many people are convinced Austin's story is pure myth, modeled after *The Legend of Sleepy Hollow*, there are some who remain certain that there might just be a whisper of truth hidden in it.

The story begins one day in late autumn as a Bostonian named Peter Rugg prepared to leave Menotomy (now known as Arlington) for a short journey into Boston, several miles away. Rugg, a horse and cattle merchant, knew the roads well and was quite familiar with this journey that many Bostonians made. He was an upstanding citizen of Boston and known for his quick wit. But, he was also known for his feisty demeanor that often propelled him to act in haste.

On this particular fall day, gray clouds began to gather, shielding what little warmth was left to be offered against the brisk autumn winds. Although the skies were overcast and the afternoon was slowly folding into night, Rugg decided to make his way home to Middle Street in Boston.

Rugg made a short stop at the home of a friend named Tom Cutter. Rugg visited to get a quick drink and warm his bones, and then made his way back outside, much to Tom Cutter's protests. Cutter thought the night was unfit for traveling and attempted to persuade

Rugg to spend the night in his house. Cutter, like Rugg, knew well the fiery disposition of a late autumn storm in New England. He pleaded with Rugg not to venture forth on the roads, spying the thickening clouds and advancing rain. But Rugg would have nothing to do with it. Even as Cutter's protestations increased, Rugg became more belligerent and shoved his friend out of the way.

Cutter relented and Rugg trudged off to his buckboard. Maybe figuring that the rain might soon let up, or feeling so incensed that he was ready to fight nature itself, Rugg hitched his horse to his carriage, placed his daughter into the back of the buckboard, and clicked his way home. Little did he know that this would be his final sojourn for, sometime during his trip, the carriage disappeared without a trace into the thick darkness of the Boston air.

Exactly what happened to Rugg, the carriage, the horse, and Rugg's daughter remains unknown to this day. Perhaps he was caught in a flash flood. Perhaps he drove his carriage off the road trying to avoid the wind driven rain. Or, perhaps somehow, the carriage was spirited away by unseen forces.

A week went by before authorities investigated the disappearance of Rugg's carriage. Investigators scanned the countryside, finding no hint of Rugg, his daughter, the carriage, or his horse. Authorities gave up the search, convinced that Rugg had vanished without a trace.

Fall turned to winter and winter, to spring. Interest in Rugg's disappearance began to wane. However, on a rainy night in May 1771, that would change as the citizens of Middle Street were awakened by a startling commotion on the streets. Several residents lit candles and tore open the shutters of their houses and one resident, the local gunsmith, noticed a glowing carriage rambling down the street. Inside it – he swore – sat Peter Rugg and his daughter.

The gunsmith, unsure of the nature of the apparition he had seen, spoke to neighbors the following day. Several other residents claimed that they, too, had spotted a ghostly carriage. Rumors abounded about the carriage and the search for information began. Other people began to step forward, claiming to have seen the former cattle dealer, his daughter, and the carriage on rainy nights throughout the land. One of the collectors at a local toll bridge was the first to come forth with such a sighting, explaining he had seen a man similar to Rugg on many a stormy night. He always flew across the bridge, eyes flaming red and temper blaring, refusing to pay the fee. A mail carrier from Newburyport claimed to see Rugg race out of a thundercloud and pursue his carriage, only to race past him, and then disappear in a flash of lightning. A ship captain, traveling by coach from Rhode Island to Boston, mentioned that he has seen a man resembling Rugg on his trip to the city. Rugg was soaked to the bone and had stopped the coach, asking the driver for directions to Boston. Once satisfied, the supposed Rugg went back into a nearby carriage, rode off, and vanished with a bolt of lightning.

Several other similar stories were passed along that mentioned a glowing carriage that appeared throughout the countryside on rainy nights in New England. Claims continued into the early eighteenth century. The last story surfaced from a preacher who was traveling by carriage to Rhode Island. As he drove through the Ocean State, the preacher noticed the weather had taken a rapid turn for the worse. Hoping to outdistance himself from a suddenly approaching thunderstorm, the preacher prodded his horse onward. The nearest town, Quonset, was but a few miles away and the preacher was certain he could arrive before the heart of the storm had overtaken him.

As the preacher's carriage edged closer to town, a wicked sound pierced the daytime. The preacher looked up and saw a carriage careening toward him in the opposite direction. The glowing vehicle sped quickly toward him. The preacher tightened the reins and shouted to the out-of-control carriage. As the carriage came closer, the preacher noticed the driver was a pasty looking man with a girl by his side. Both appeared petrified and uncertain of what lay ahead as they raced toward the preacher's carriage.

The preacher pleaded one more time for the carriage to stop. A moment later, the preacher's horse reared up. A flash of light illuminated the surrounding air as a rush of wind blew past the preacher. The preacher was sent hurtling through the air, landing on the ground in a cold faint.

When the preacher came too, he shook his head and noticed that the skies had cleared. He rubbed his aching head, wondering if he had been dreaming. Then, he looked to the side of the road and saw the distinct outline of hoof prints branded into the rocks at the side of the road, made by a horse that was surely not his.

The preacher took off from the site, never to return to the spot again. He told others of the frightful encounter and soon they were all convinced that the preacher had an encounter with the once forgotten Peter Rugg.

Curiosity abounded for weeks after the preacher's incident. People flocked to the region of Quonset, seeking out the hoof prints, certain to get a clue about Rugg's disappearance. Yet, Peter Rugg was never heard from again.

Did he find peace with his final encounter with a member of the clergy? Or did he finally find his way back to Boston, nearly fifty years after he first set foot? The world may never know.

In the days since the story, Middle Street has succumbed to the expansion of the city. The spot where Rugg once lived is now near the North End of Boston, where other ghostly visitors have been spotted. Middle Street has become Hanover Street. Perhaps because the street his house once rested on no longer exists, Mr. Rugg has found a new city to call home.

William Mumler once practiced spirit photography in the heart of Boston.
Did ghosts once roam these Beacon Hill streets, in search of his studio?

The Famous Spirit Photographer

The Strange Tale of William Mumler...

The History

I n the late 1800s and early 1900s, spiritualism became popular in the United States. People hoping to have contact with departed loved ones flocked to psychic specialists called mediums.

Many cities had mediums during the height of spiritualism and Boston was no stranger to the spiritual world. Numerous mediums set up shop throughout the city. Some served as mere peddlers, passing through town hoping to share their insight into "the other world," and quickly move on. Others proved to be charlatans posing as mediums. They hoped to gain a quick dollar through chicanery.

Then there was a group of mediums who gave pause to America. Even to this day, there are historians, scientists, and Americans who wonder if these mediums truly had paranormal abilities. William Mumler was one such person. He was no ordinary spiritualist. Instead, he was a spirit photographer who had the ability to capture the essence of the deceased on a piece of film.

The idea of spirit photography first evolved in the 1860s. Although often attributed to Mumler, the first true spirit photograph was mostly likely taken in 1860 by a man named W. Campbell who lived in New Jersey. While trying to take a sample photograph of an empty chair, Campbell noticed he had also captured the image of a small boy on film when he developed the picture. Campbell had no clue who the boy was. He was unable to create such a photograph again and his thoughts on the matter seem to have disappeared into history.

Mumler is credited with popularizing the idea of spirit photography from his Washington Street home in 1861. Mumler was an engraver by trade, but enjoyed amateur photography in his free time. Because photography was a new art form, Mumler frequently experimented with it. One day, while photographing himself, he noticed a strange figure of a woman appeared on one of his final prints. While look-ing closely at the picture, Mumler thought the figure resembled his cousin who had died twelve years prior to the photograph. Mumler remembered feeling a strange sensation when taking the picture, but thought nothing of it at the time.

Mumler's photograph soon caught the attention of the spirit world. Mediums and other spiritualists flocked to see the picture. Some thought Mumler's photograph was a hoax. Mumler denied that anyone was in the room and adamantly claimed that the photograph was real. Mumler's claim sparked intense interest in spiritual photog-raphy and soon people flocked to his home requesting he take their pictures, with the hopes that a loved one might show up as well. In time, Mumler abandoned his engraving job at a local jeweler and dedicated his time to taking photographs of anyone who wanted to purchase them.

Skepticism abounded and one of Boston's prominent photog-raphers, William Black, investigated Mumler's ability to capture "spirits." Black sat in on one of Mumler's photo shoots and studied his every move carefully. Everything Mumler did, from shooting the picture to developing the film followed the procedures of the day. Black had Mumler take his picture and Black himself developed it. Much to Black's surprise, the picture of himself included another person — the figure of a man standing behind him. Black had no idea how the spirit got there and could offer no explanation for the appearance of the figure.

After Black's investigation, Mumler became an even more popular spiritual photographer in Boston. His pictures sometimes had startling images of what looked like ghosts and other apparitions, though most had just faint images in the background. Despite investigations by Black, as well as a New York judge named John Edmonds who eventually became a Mumler supporter, critics considered Mumler a fraud. He left Boston and went to New York in 1869.

The Mystery

Mumler's ghostly photographs remain a mystery to this day. Scientists and authorities at the time found no proof that he was enhancing pictures in any way. Yet, rumors to the effect persisted, particularly after Mumler moved to New York.

While in New York, Mumler took his most famous spirit picture. A lady named Mrs. Tydall (or Mrs. Tundall, depending on the source) dressed in black and wearing a veil, arrived at his studio. Although she did not have an appointment, she asked Mumler to take her photograph. Mumler obliged and led her to a chair in his studio. While he prepared the film, he noticed that Mrs. Tydall still wore her veil. When he inquired if she planned to wear it in the photograph, Mrs. Tydall explained that she would remove it when he was ready to shoot the picture.

Right before Mumler took the picture, the customer removed her veil. When Mumler developed the picture, a strange thing happened. A shadowy figure emerged from the depths of the photograph. It bore an uncanny resemblance to former President Abraham Lincoln.

Undoubtedly, Mumler was perplexed. What would Lincoln have to do with Mrs. Tydall? He soon found out as he examined the picture closely and realized that Mrs. Tydall was no Mrs. Tydall at all. She was really Mary Todd Lincoln, who had a keen interest in the supernatural and seances.

Mumler continued to take his photographs as he had done in Boston. However, he soon met the same fate. Critics pounced on his practice, charging him with fraud. The mayor of New York even had Mumler arrested and put on trial.

During the trial, several witnesses spoke on Mumler's behalf. Many experts also took the stand having investigated Mumler's photographs and his process of capturing real and supernatural images. No one could find any proof of treachery on Mumler's part. Mumler was eventually acquitted

To this day, no one is exactly sure what to make of Mumler's photographs, including Mumler himself, who tried to find a reason for the strange shadows that emerged onto his pictures. Eventually, the spiritual photographer from Boston and New York faded into the background of history, much like many of the images he captured. His popularity waned as criticism lingered. Some historians think Mumler may have been onto something with his early photographs, but began using some camera trickery in his later ones.

Either way, an important question still lingers. Were there spirits that came to Boston (and later New York) hoping to be captured on film for an eternity? And, if so, why did they chose Mumler? Unfortunately, the answers to these questions, too, have faded like an old photograph over time. It is possible that, one day, they will resurface in the simple flash of a camera.

Resources

A wealth of fabulous material abounds relating to the ghosts and cemeteries of Boston. The following books, articles, and websites proved quite helpful in providing interesting information about the ghost stories contained in this volume. The books, in particular, were highly valuable for their insights and information. I would recommend them to all ghost enthusiasts.

Books

Bahne, Charles. *The Complete Guide to Boston's Freedom Trail*. Cambridge, Massachusetts: Newtowne Publishing, 1993.

Barber, John Warner. Historical connections. *Being a General Collection of Interesting Facts, Traditions, Biographical Sketches, Anecdotes relating to the History and Antiquities of Every Town in Massachusetts*. 1844. Retrieved online at Google books.

Cahill, Robert Ellis. *Lighthouse Mysteries of the North Atlantic*. Salem, Massachusetts: Old Saltbox Publishing House, 1998.

Mont, Joseph & Weaver, Marcia. *Ghosts of Boston*. Boston, Massachusetts: Snakehead Press, 2002.

Nadler, Holly Mascott. *Ghosts of Boston Town: Three Centuries of True Hauntings*. Camden, Maine: Downeast Books, 2002.

Rossiter, William. *Old Ways and Old Days of Boston*. Boston, Massachusetts: R.H. Sterns. 1915. Retrieved online at Google books.

Sammons, Mary Beth & Edwards, Robert. *City Ghosts: True Tales of Hauntings in America's Cities*. New York, New York: Sterling Publishing, 2006.

Snow, Edward Rowe & D'Entremont, Jeremy. *The Islands of Boston Harbor* (Snow Centennial Editions). Beverly, Massachusetts: Commonwealth Editions, 2002.

Steitz, George. *Haunted Lighthouses*. Sarasota, Florida: Pineapple Press, 2002.

Stevens, Austin N. (ed). *Mysterious New England*. Camden, Maine: Yankee Books, 1971.

Online periodicals

Albert, Michael, Ostheimer, Kristen, Liewehr, David, Steiberg, Seth, & Breman, Joel. "Smallpox Manifestations and Survival during the Boston Epidemic of 1901 to 1903." *Annals of Internal Medicine*, December 17, 2002.

Beste, Meg. "Boston's Haunted." *The Heights* (Boston College newspaper), October 31, 2005. Retrieved at http://media.www.bcheights.com/media/storage/paper144/news/2005/10/31/Features/Bostons.Haunted-1039397.shtml

Craig, David. "Who's behind the building?" *B.U. Bridge*. October 15, 1999. Retrieved: http://www.bu.edu/bridge/archive/1999/10-15/features8.html

D'Entremont, Jeremy. "The Darker Side of Boston Harbor's Lighthouses." *Lighthouse Digest*. October 2000. Retrieved at http://www.lighthousedepot.com/digest/Storypage.cfm?storykey=863

D'Entremont, Jeremy. "Nix's Mate "Ominous and Sinister" DayBeacon Overhauled." *Lighthouse Digest*. Retrieved at www.lighthousedepot.com/digest/StoryPage.cfm?StoryKey=1830

Fitzgerald, Brian. "B.U. Prof's course anchored in Boston Harbor." *B.U. Bridge*. Vol II, No. 17 December 11 1998 - January 7- 1999. Retrieved at http://www.bu.edu/bridge/archive/1998/12-11/features7.html

"The Iceman Stayeth: Eugene O'Neill's ghost a permanent resident of Shelton Hall?" *B.U. Bridge*. October 29, 1999. Retrieved at http://www.bu.edu/bridge/archive/1999/10-29/features4.html

Klimetz, Julianne. "Babe Ruth, Boston Strangler may haunt dorms." *The Daily Free Press: The Independent Student Newspaper at Boston University*. October 31, 2003. Retrieved: http://media. www.dailyfreepress.com/media/storage/paper87/news/2003/10/31/News/Babe-Ruth.Boston. Strangler.May.Haunt.Dorms-545390.shtml

May, Patrick. "Diaria, Let's take a tour through Boston University." *The Daily Free Press: The Independent Student Newspaper at Boston University*. February 18, 2004. Retrieved at http://media.www. dailyfreepress.com/media/storage/paper87/news/2004/02/18/Opinion/Diaria.Lets.Take.A.Tour. Through.Boston.University-610789.shtml

O'Shea, Joe. "A spirited tour of Boston." Originally appearing in *AAA Horizons*. Written by Joe O'Shea. Retrieved from O'Shea Communications Writing Portfolio. http://www.joeoshea.net/write/samples/ aaa_bostonspirits.html

"What Lies Beneath." Retrieved: http://www.panoramamagazine.com/panoramamagazine/articles/ what_lies_beneath.

Websites

Note: websites are arranged by book chapter for easy reference.

Myles Standish Hall. http://en.wikipedia.org/wiki/Myles_Standish_Hall

The Boston Athenaeum website. www.bostonathenaeum.org/
    wikipedia.org/wiki/Boston_Athenaeum
    http://www.answers.com/topic/boston-athen-um

New England ghost tours. http://www.newenglandghosttours.com/tours.html

Ziptrivia: Boston Ghost to Coast. http://ziptrivia.com/play/boston_ghost_to_coast/theme/boo_to_you

Massachusetts Haunting. http://www.ratrun.com/massachusetts.htm

Haunted America. http //www.leftfield-psi.net/ghosts/haunted_places/usa_m.html

"The Story Behind Charlesgate." http://www.dinakeratsis.com/CGhistory.htm

History of the Cutler Majestic Theater. http://www.maj.org/historyindex.html

Top Haunted Spots. boston.citysearch.com/roundup/40468

Massachusetts Haunted Travel. http://www.ghosttraveller.com/Massachusetts.htm

The Boston Commons and Other Famous Hauntings in Boston, Massachusetts. A Ghostly Guide to Boston's Sprit World. By Sherri Granato. http://www.associatedcontent.com/article/73853/the_boston_commons_and_other_famous.html?page=3

Massachusetts Paranormal Crossroads. http://www.masscrossroads.com/
    The Charlesgate Hotel. http://www.masscrossroads.com/cgate.html
    The Emerson Majestic. http://www.masscrossroads.com/maj

Haunted Hotel: The Omni Parker House by Charlyn Keating Chisholm. http://hotels.about.com/od/ hauntedhotels/p/hau_omniparker.htm

Omni Parker House: A Brief History. http://www.omnihotels.com/upload/images/hotels/bospar/pdf/bospar_history%20book%20pages.pdf.

BU Yesterday; http://web.bu.edu/today/snapshots/yesterday.shtml

Chilly Stories of Boston University. The Catacombs of Shelton Hall. http://www.chillystories.com/Catacombs.htm

Boston Lighthouse History. http://lighthouse.cc/boston/history.html

Boston Odyssey Cruises. www.odysseycruises.com/ boston/about_ship/cruise_route.cfm

Long Wharf Investors Origin of Name. http://www.long-wharf.com/name_origin.html

"Hunting New England Shipwrecks." http://www.wreckhunter.net/mawrecks.htm

"Description of Le Magnifique." *New England Explorations.com*. http://www.newenglandexplorations. com/bostonharborproject/magnifique.html

"Gallops Island." http://en.wikipedia.org/wiki/Gallops_Island

"Gallop's Island." Boston Harbor Visitor's Guide. http://www.bostonislands.org/isle_gallops.html

"Gallop Island Facts." Boston Harbor Islands - Island Factsheet. http://www.bostonislands.org/factsheet_template.asp?rsIslands__MMColParam=gall

"George's Island: A Short History." http://www.bostonislands.org/isle_georges_history.html

"Four Centuries of Boston History." http://members.aol.com/UniqueCitiTours/Boston/Chronology.pdf.
"Long Island, Massachusetts." http://en.wikipedia.org/wiki/Long_Island_(Massachusetts)
Nixes Mate Fact Sheet. http://www.bostonislands.org/factsheet_template.asp?rsIslands__
    MMColParam=nima
Maritime History of Massachusetts: Nix's Mate Daybeacon. http://www.cr.nps.gov/nr/travel/maritime/
    nix.htm
THE ISLANDS OF BOSTON HARBOUR. http://kellscraft.com/EventsBoston/EventsBoston04.html
"William Fly." http://en.wikipedia.org/wiki/William_Fly
The North End: Boston, Massachusetts. http://www.revolutionaryday.com/usroute20/northend/default.
    htm
King's Chapel Burying Ground. http://www.graveaddiction.com/kingch.html
"Kings Chapel and Burying Ground. Celebrate Boston. http://www.celebrateboston.com/sites/king-
    schapel.htm
"Fort Warren on George's Island." Information Navigation. http://www.infonavigate.com/boston/121.
    htm
"History of Fort Warren." http://home.comcast.net/~jay.schmidt/ft.warren/
"The Lady in Black." http://home.comcast.net/~jay.schmidt/ft.warren/ghost.html
History of Spirit Photography. www.prairieghosts.com/ph_history.html
"Haunted Places in Massachusetts." www.juiceenewsdaily.com/0105/news/haunted_massachusetts.
    html
"Where even the ghosts known your name." A review of Cheers Beacon Hill by Adrienne Foster. http://
    www.epinions.com/content_184136863364
Citizen Information Service. Massachusetts Facts: Concise Facts Part One. http://www.sec.state.
    ma.us/cis/cismaf/mf1c.htm
Celebrate Boston. Central Burying Ground. http://www.celebrateboston.com/sites/centralburyingground.
    htm
Boston University Theater. http://www.huntingtontheatre.org/venue/but.aspx
The Freedom Trail. Copp's Hill Burying Ground. http://www.nps.gov/archive/bost/bost_lographics/cop-
    phill.htm

Index